MAKING (ALMOST)

INSTANT
PUPPETS

MAKING (ALMOST)

INSTANT PUPPETS

DAVID CURRELL

THE CROWOOD PRESS

CONTENTS

INTRODUCTION

Puppets hold a fascination that embraces all ages and cultures. The slightest tilt of the head, a hand gesture, or a stillness can have a powerful effect, inviting the audience to interpret additional dimensions, just as we 'see' characters in a book or a radio play.

For thousands of years people have animated inanimate objects in a dramatic manner for many purposes and puppets continue to be used for religious rites, entertainment, satire, education, propaganda, advertising and therapy. In recent years, puppet theatre has reaffirmed its status as an art form worthy of consideration by adults as well as children, and puppets can now be seen alongside actors on the professional stage.

The puppets can be as simple or as complicated as required and there are times when we need to see results quickly, so this book is intended for those who want to create puppets with limited time or resources, in an hour or two, a day, or a weekend.

They may be for a solo, group or family activity; for inclusion and diversity in the school curriculum; for creativity or problem solving; for therapy where the focus may be the construction or the 'performance'; for drama workshops; for larger projects where quickly made figures facilitate rehearsals while the actual puppets are being made; or for *object theatre* in which objects can become characters themselves.

Nearly all the puppets in this book have been made by people with little or no previous experience of making puppets. Familiar household tools were used and very few materials were bought. Cartons, containers, packaging, fabric remnants and other items were used that would otherwise be recycled or binned. Please use this book to understand the principles and techniques of puppet making, upcycle whatever materials are available, experiment and be inventive.

CHAPTER 1

DIFFERENT TYPES OF PUPPET

Three-dimensional puppets tend to be characterised by the method of operation, most often by a hand, rod(s) or strings. Hand puppets and rod puppets have a hand or rod as their central core for support, so these are direct methods of manipulation. Marionettes, or string puppets, are usually manipulated from a short distance above by threads attached to a control.

Hand puppets and rod puppets tend to go where the performer puts them, whereas marionettes have a little more of a life of their own on the end of the strings. All these methods have variations that sometimes involve combinations such as hand-and-rods or strings-and-rods.

Shadow puppets are normally flat, cut-out shapes performed with natural or artificial light to cast shadows, usually onto a screen. Three-dimensional figures and even actors can be used for shadow play, but they need a strong light source to achieve sharp shadows.

HAND PUPPETS

Hand puppets differ in the extent to which the puppeteer's hand or arm is inserted into the figure.

Finger puppets are the simplest form of hand puppet. They are often a tube-like shape slipped onto a finger or a shape representing a head slipped onto a fingertip but there are many variations.

Glove puppets, used like a glove on the puppeteer's hand, can handle objects and are good for fast, robust movement. You can operate one on each hand, which increases their scope, but

Quickly made and easily manipulated, finger puppets are wonderful for storytelling; a whole puppet family can fit on one hand.

OPPOSITE: The Devil, a mixture of string puppet and shadow figure, by Jonathan Hayter, Figure of Speech Puppet Company.

it is not easy making a 'glove' body that fits well and is comfortable. Other types of puppet might be more suitable for children with tiny hands. It is often better to make a basic glove onto which the costume is added, rather than making the glove from the costume itself. Using draped material will be much quicker than making the traditional glove.

Sleeve puppets have a head and a longer body so your whole arm fits inside, with the hand operating the head and, possibly, a moving mouth. These can be much larger than glove puppets and, depending on their size, you could operate two of these at the same time. If you choose to use your free hand as the puppet's hand, then you are restricted to one puppet per puppeteer.

ROD PUPPETS

Rod puppets are frequently controlled from below or behind. They may be very basic figures, sometimes no more than a wooden spoon, but they are usually more substantial with arms and hands controlled by rods or stiff wires operated by the puppeteer's free hand. It is common for rod puppets not to have legs and feet but to perform behind a screen where they are visible to their waist or hips.

A rod puppet with a long central rod can be held up high and can be quite large if required, which helps with sightlines and visibility for a large audience, provided it is not too heavy. One disadvantage of a long central rod is the puppet cannot bend at the waist, so it is somewhat limited in its range of movements.

A rod puppet with a short central rod has flexibility at the waist and enjoys a greater range

A hand puppet with a well-fitting 'glove' body, upon which a costume can be added.

A costumed human hand gives the puppet considerable scope.

A rod puppet with a draped costume, which is quick and easy to create. It needs no legs and feet – a common feature of rod puppets.

of movements, but it cannot be held as high as one with a long rod.

Sometimes rod puppets are controlled from above. This is particularly suitable for animal characters where very direct control is needed, possibly alongside marionettes.

Two-person operation increases the scope of rod puppets and invites cooperation and coordination. One person may control the head/body rod and one of the hands while a second person operates the other hand. Alternatively, the second person might control both hands.

Table-top rod puppets are similar to the traditional Japanese *Bunraku* style of presentation that has three operators to each main figure. The modern version is often smaller in scale, with the puppets manipulated at table height, whether on a stage surface or operated in the air; with skilful manipulation you feel you can 'see' the surface, even when there is none.

A table-top puppet can be operated by one, two or possibly three puppeteers, as necessary, but its size may determine how many puppeteers is feasible.

Control by a combination of hands and rods is common. Hand puppets may be operated by a hand in the head while rods control the hands (a hand-and-rod puppet), or a rod puppet may have human hands (a rod-and-hand puppet). Similarly, strings and rods (or wires) may be combined in the control of what are often called rod-marionettes.

Pierrot, by the late Barry Smith's Theatre of Puppets, was designed to be operated by three puppeteers.

Orlando Furioso, a Sicilian rod-marionette, has rods to the head and sword arm, and a string to the shield arm. The legs are controlled through the momentum created by the head rod.

MARIONETTES

The term 'marionette' can have different meanings. In some countries marionette simply means 'puppet' and the international puppetry association, *L'Union Internationale de la Marionnette*, is inclusive of all types of puppet. In English-speaking countries, it is more often used for string puppets.

Marionettes that are string puppets may have less direct control than other puppets, but they can adopt almost any position. They are not well suited to fast, robust, forceful movements but they can twist, turn, move gracefully, even defy gravity and fly through the air. They are generally regarded as the most complicated type of puppet to operate but well-balanced marionettes have built-in movement, like a pendulum; with a suitable control, they do a lot of the work for you.

Very simple controls require the operator to pull individual strings to achieve the required actions, but a slightly more complicated arrangement enables the puppet to move effectively just by tilting and turning the control.

Tangles need not be problematic if a control is dropped; the trick is to pick up the control gently, *not* the puppet, and undo any loose tangles without taking the weight of the puppet as this might pull a loose tangle into a knot.

SHADOW PUPPETS

Shadow puppets can range from simple cut-out cardboard shapes to colourful leather figures with intricate designs. Depending on the materials and techniques used, a shadow puppet is one of the quickest types of puppet to make and

Eight strings support and operate this marionette. It has extra strings for moving the eyes and mouth, playing a piano and raising his hat.

A shadow puppet created by Lotte Reiniger, one of the early creators of animated films. She drew rough proportions on the card and did most of the shaping with scissors.

even roughly cut shapes can look surprisingly delicate on the shadow screen. It is remarkable how even beautifully made shadow puppets often have a greater impact as shadows than they do when viewed without the screen.

The puppets are frequently controlled by a rod or stiff wire from below or behind, though it is possible to hang them on threads. Often performers require a method that keeps the puppet tight to the screen, but the nature and position of the light source will also influence the angle of operation.

Simple shadow puppets may be just a cardboard shape in which the outline has been drawn and then cut out. Lotte Reiniger, who created the first feature-length animated shadow puppet film, would scribble a rough shape on the card and then use small, sharp scissors to create the detail as she cut.

Jointed shadow puppets may have many moving parts, with control often achieved indirectly through the main control. Controls attached to the head and/or body, hands and legs require very skilful operation; in inexperienced hands or with two-person control, damage often occurs, so it is better to have one main control and add one additional control only if it is essential. With a little practice you can achieve considerable control by the way you move the figure against the screen.

Cut-out designs are used to enhance the character, and colour and texture with both solid and translucent materials may also be added to the cut-out designs.

Coloured and oiled card is the modern equivalent to the traditional Asian and oriental shadow puppets for which leather was treated to make it translucent, designs were cut in the surface, and colour was added with dyes. This technique has been adapted to make full-colour shadows quickly using felt pens or inks on white card.

A Turkish shadow puppet made from leather. It is translucent with cut-out designs and coloured with dyes. Parallel techniques with decoration and colour are described in Chapter 7.

CHAPTER 2

MATERIALS, TOOLS, HEADS AND COSTUMES

RECYCLED MATERIALS

Many containers that are useful for making instant puppets are already shaped in ways that may suggest heads, features or bodies. These items were designed not just for their functionality but also to attract shoppers, so they often have inbuilt potential for puppets. Whatever materials are used for making a puppet, ensure that the finished puppet is as clean and attractive as possible, unless the characterisation requires otherwise.

It is a good idea to have a collection of empty containers of all kinds and to sort them into labelled boxes. When selecting a container for a particular purpose, consider whether it is strong enough in itself or whether it needs a supporting structure inside it.

Keep off-cuts of wood, rods and tubing, whether cardboard, plastic, foam rubber or even metal. Galvanised wire (coat-hanger wire) and other types of wire are useful for joints, controls and shaping of flexible materials. Blocks of foam rubber and other packaging from boxed items are useful for making puppet parts or for padding other items to the required shape, and sponges can become heads, features or bodies.

The shapes of cartons and containers immediately suggest all manner of heads and bodies.

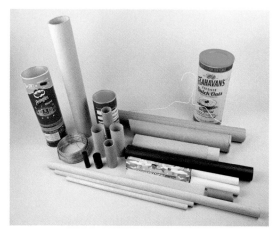

Rods and tubing are quickly turned into a range of body parts or limbs, as well as controls.

Lightweight materials in blocks or layers give puppets shape without making them heavy.

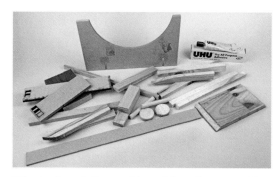

Off-cuts of wood often provide a solid core for a puppet, its limbs and controls.

Note: *Although there are examples of polystyrene blocks being used, it is not generally recommended where any significant shaping is required. Breathing the particles from dry shaping or the fumes from hot-wire shaping is a health hazard which should be avoided.*

Ropes, cords and twine, ranging from thick and heavy to very fine, may be used for joints, hair, sometimes in place of arms and legs, and for control strings. When threading a cord through a small hole, a darning needle with a large eye is useful. If the ends of the cord are loose, wrap a small piece of masking tape around, and just over, the end and twist it into a point.

Fabrics, remnants, old socks and clothes that young children have outgrown are very useful. Dolls' clothes are usually unsuitable because they restrict movement. Old leather or suede leather garments are handy for joints and trimmings. Make separate collections of things that may be useful for hair, eyes and other features.

From fine thread to thick rope, there is something useful for almost every puppet.

Materials in all sizes are invaluable; even small pieces find a use.

Colourful buttons, beads and balls have various applications, not just eyes and costumes; matching pairs are especially useful.

Balls and beads of all sizes will be useful for puppet parts and for helping to create smooth joints. Interesting-looking buttons are ideal for creating facial features as well as enhancing costumes. Simple buttons help with attaching control strings and rods and sometimes with making joints; they need to be secured firmly to avoid risk of detaching.

Wools, embroidery threads, string, rope, fur, feathers and tissue paper are examples of materials useful for hair and other trimmings.

The way hair shapes the head and frames the face can change a puppet completely.

Materials for Shadow Puppets

Reasonably stiff cardboard, such as a cereal or detergent box, is suitable for opaque shadow puppets and cut-out designs. For shadows in full-colour, good-quality white card (such as Ivory Board) is required. In order to protect all surfaces while cutting, a self-healing cutting mat is a good investment as it will be useful when making all types of puppet.

Further suggestions for useful materials are detailed in Chapter 7, Shadow Puppets.

The materials suitable for shadow screens include polyester cotton fabric (an old sheet), shower curtain material (preferably plain), grease-proof paper/baking paper, artists' or architects' tracing paper, or tracing linen is even better. If you are lucky enough to find a theatre with pieces of unwanted rear-screen projection material, this is ideal. However, the shadow screens in this book used nothing more than a shower curtain and, mostly, greaseproof paper from the kitchen, so do not feel the need to purchase expensive material.

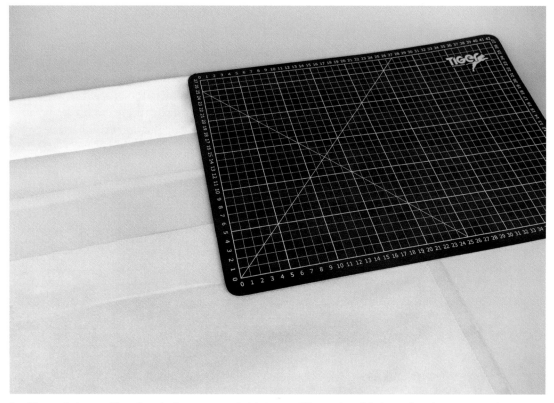

A cutting mat, shown with various shadow screen materials, is one of the most useful pieces of equipment to purchase.

TOOLS

The tools that one might find in a household toolbox are often sufficient for most instant puppet projects and you could manage with fewer than those illustrated here. You may not need chisels, but the odd screwdriver may be handy along with large and small pliers, a tack hammer, a selection of brushes, a measuring tape and a try square or a set square.

There are certain items that are not so common but are particularly useful to acquire:

- A paper drill that has interchangeable heads for different-size holes; always use it with a strip of wood or MDF underneath to protect other surfaces (a stationery punch is an alternative but this limits where a hole can be positioned and its size).
- A de-burring tool that can be used to enlarge holes in a wide variety of materials (*see* overleaf).
- A fine, round file (and a flat file is often useful too).
- An awl or other tool with a sharp point.

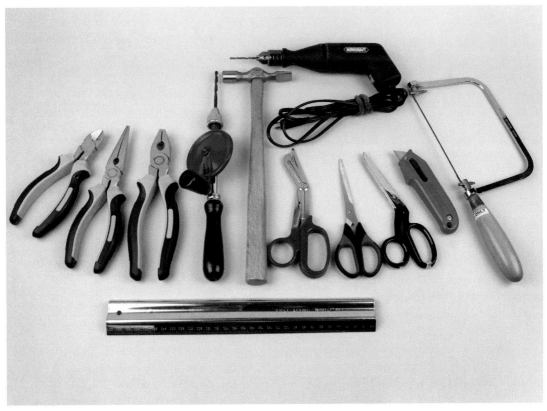

Each of these household tools was used during the making of the puppets but it is not necessary to have all of them.

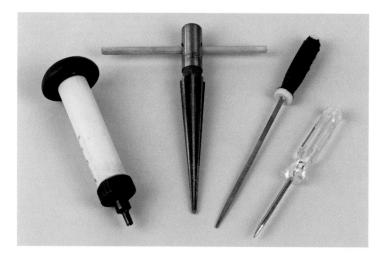

These tools proved useful in making many of the puppets, especially the de-burring tool for enlarging holes. Left to right: paper drill, de-burring tool, round file, any sharp pointed tool.

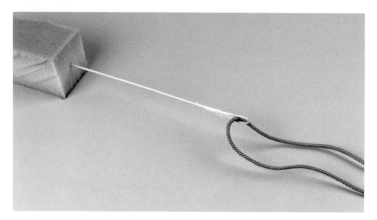

Occasionally improvisation is required, for example when you need a very long needle with a large eye.

Keep the tools clean, sharp where appropriate, and use them for their intended purpose to preserve their usefulness and for reasons of safety.

To thread cord through any large object or a solid block of foam rubber or polystyrene, cut a length of coat-hanger wire and bend the end into a loop to make it into a long needle. Taping the closure of the loop is not essential but it helps to prevent it catching inside the object.

Note: *It is strongly recommended that you wear an apron, other protective clothing or old clothes when cutting, shaping or gluing the puppet parts. It is easy for a large spot of glue to drop unnoticed onto a skirt or trousers or for a rough edge of a container to snag a jumper, so always dress appropriately to protect your clothes from mishap.*

Cutting

Always protect any surface with a cutting mat unless you are using a work bench.

It is desirable to have at least two pairs of scissors so that you do not cut fabric with scissors used for paper or card.

It is a mistake to try to cut large pieces of foam rubber with scissors as foam rubber is more resistant than it appears. An old bread knife, a hacksaw blade, or pulling and tearing pieces off, is much more suitable for the general shaping; if necessary, use scissors for snipping away at the surface for the final shaping.

Craft knives with replaceable blades – one with wide blades and one with finer blades like a scalpel – are among the most useful cutting tools. A metal safety ruler with a finger groove for safe cutting is recommended. When using a knife, never cut towards the hand holding the item being cut.

A coping saw and a junior hacksaw will cover most other cutting requirements but a tenon saw would be a bonus.

Tin cans and cut edges in plastic bottles may need protecting with a little foam rubber or masking tape, especially if fingers or hands are to be inserted into them.

Drilling

To make small holes or to start a hole for a drill-bit to grip, an awl or other sharp pointed object can be used. Alternatives are a bradawl or gimlet, but you could manage with any pointed tool. A de-burring tool is particularly useful when you want to enlarge a hole gradually.

You may not need to do much drilling, so a power drill may not be needed, but a hand drill is useful to have, with a variety of twist drills and spade drills (or points).

Shaping

While a rasp or files are useful, for most of the puppets included in this book a few grades of glass paper were sufficient. Large corners in wood can be removed with a saw, and glass-paper around a sanding block can be used to round off or smooth any uneven patches.

To hold items while shaping, drilling or other work on them, a vice with wooden jaws is desirable, either permanently attached to a workbench or one that can be clamped to any suitable work surface.

Please note the warning above about cutting foam rubber. The same issue applies to shaping it.

ADHESIVES

It is always a good idea to test any adhesive on a small, inconspicuous part of the surfaces or materials with which you plan to use it as some adhesives will eat into or dissolve certain materials. To improve adhesion on shiny surfaces, it may help to roughen them with glasspaper first.

Strong contact glues like UHU and Bostik are very useful as general, all-purpose adhesives, as is PVA or wood glue. Copydex or special fabric adhesive is often recommended for joining together pieces of cloth, but UHU and Bostik work well and quickly on many fabrics.

The term 'foam rubber' is used loosely to cover many types of sponge or foam packaging with different constituents that respond differently to certain adhesives. UHU or Bostik are often useful with such materials, but it is best to test it first as these adhesives will dissolve some foams. They also eat away at polystyrene, so try PVA as an alternative.

Adhesive tape is useful for some joints or making hinges (for example, elbows or knees); masking tape or duct tape is preferable to Sellotape, which is not recommended.

If a joint or attachment needs reinforcement, strong adhesive tape, or a fabric strip glued on, may serve the purpose but a few stitches with a strong thread and a large-eyed needle, such as a darning needle, may be helpful.

HEADS

Heads can be made from a variety of items, some with very little alteration, but it is important to consider the structure of the whole puppet and not plan the head in isolation. Joints between each part of the puppet depend upon what those parts are made from, what actions the puppet will perform and what type of puppet it will be. Marionettes, for example, need some form of secure fixture around ear-height for fastening head strings, and a rod puppet with a nodding head will have different requirements from one with a turning head.

Some puppets are little more than a head, possibly used with a gloved hand or with a simple draped piece of material. In such instances, almost the entire puppet is described when detailing the head. In future chapters this is not repeated but is cross-referenced when describing the whole figure and any alternative ways of using it.

Improvised Heads

A combination of materials can produce interesting heads. The character illustrated was created by gluing together two scraps of foam rubber and adding two hair bobbles joined by a piece of wire. The wire was made into a loop to hold or insert a finger to operate it. It could become a person or a bird.

A ball of any type offers a basis for many sizes of puppet head. The ball may be adapted to accommodate fingers for hand puppets, dowel rods or tubing for a rod puppet, or a short dowel as a neck for a marionette.

A dish mop quickly becomes the head of a rod puppet if the mop is tied up to create hair. The minimum of features is needed. Opposite rivet-type paper fasteners serve as eyes, so we recognise a face.

Foam rubber and plastic balls from a hair accessory are transformed into a head.

A simple ball on a finger quickly finds a personality.

A pair of eyes is all the dish mop needs to become a character.

A sponge can be made into a puppet head or features with little change to its form. The shape of a sponge may suggest a particular character; try turning it sideways or inverting it to see how the character might change or possibly suggest an animal.

Invert the sponge and see how it changes character.

Hand Puppet Heads

A fabric finger puppet

A finger puppet can be slipped on top of a draped rod to become a rod puppet too.

Materials: a strip of paper, piece of felt or fur fabric, clear contact adhesive or a suitable alternative.

1. Make a template by rolling a strip of paper around your finger with a little overlap of no more than 1cm. It should be a good fit. If you plan to use the finger puppet on a gloved hand, make any template around the glove with your hand inside it.
2. Use this strip of paper to mark the width on a piece of felt or fur fabric that is a little more than the height of your finger.
3. Cut out the fabric and curl it around your finger to check the size. If it is satisfactory, note where the overlap ends and glue along the overlapping edge of the fabric to form a tube to fit onto your finger.
4. Add features, hair or accessories as required.

A conical finger puppet

This finger puppet is essentially a head made from a cardboard cone that sits on your finger.

Materials: a piece of cardboard, small pieces of felt, clear contact adhesive or a suitable alternative.

1. Cut a circle of cardboard with the radius the same length as you want the head to be. Make two cuts along the radius to the centre of the circle to remove an arc.
2. Curl the card into a cone to fit the finger to be used. Make sure it is a good fit and mark the overlap. Leave sufficient overlap for good adhesion and cut away any surplus.

3. Glue along the overlapping part and press firmly but carefully over the matching edge. While the glue is drying, hold the cone in place with a clothes peg or a strong paper clip.
4. Add features as required; the example shown has ears made from two pieces of coloured felt glued inside the cone, and stuck-on eyes and nose.
5. Insert your finger to operate the cone.

A finger puppet made in a similar way, but with a moving mouth, is described in Chapter 4.

The first step in making a cone for a finger puppet head: an arc is cut from a circle of card.

The cardboard cone is curled, glued and held securely while the glue sets.

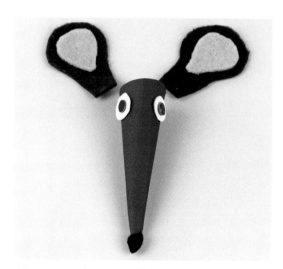

Felt ears are ready to be glued inside the cone; circles punched from cardboard are the eyes; a small part of a fluffy ball is the nose.

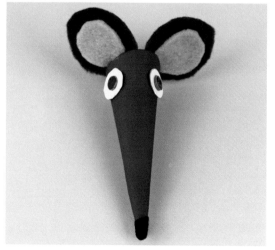

The cone head is assembled ready for use. The performer's hand will become its body.

A sock head

To make an old sock into a hand puppet:

1. Insert your hand inside it in the operating position with fingers together on top and thumb underneath.
2. Tuck the sock into the required shape between your thumb and the fingers, to look like a mouth.
3. Add any features you might require. This puppet head has red felt to line the mouth and funny self-adhesive eyes.

An old sock, a strip of felt and self-adhesive 'wiggly' eyes are ready for transformation into a puppet.

The toe of the sock is tucked in between fingers and thumb to form the mouth.

Alternatively, the sock may be stuffed with a ball, foam rubber, paper or fabric to form the head for a glove puppet, rod puppet or marionette. (*See* the section 'A ball head for a marionette' later in this chapter.)

A paper plate sleeve puppet

Materials: cardboard picnic plate, cardboard, fabric tube (for example a sleeve or a leg from old clothes), trimmings.

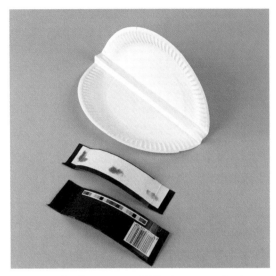

The paper plate has a zig-zag fold in the centre to let the mouth open wider.

1. Fold the centre of the picnic plate into the zig-zag shape illustrated. A single fold will give a little mouth movement, but the zig-zag fold enables the mouth to open wider.
2. Bend two strips of card into arched shapes and glue one on the top and one on the bottom of the folded plate.

Glue the cardboard strips in loops that fit your hand comfortably without being loose.

3. Pad the top and bottom of the plate to the required shape with part of another paper plate, glued on. Of course, you can use any other padding you wish to create the head shape.

   When the puppet is complete, insert your hand to operate the head and move the mouth.

4. Choose a suitable piece of fabric tube to cover the head and form the body. You can make a tube of fabric, but it is quicker to use an arm or a leg from unwanted clothing. If it is too wide, you can gather it in but, ideally, it needs to be just over twice as wide as the plate and a little longer than from your fingertips to your elbow.

5. Put the plate in the end of the sleeve and fold the material over it to cover the inside edge of the mouth. Glue the fabric to the plate, using clothes pegs or paper clips to hold it in place while drying.

6. Glue a lining into the mouth to cover the edges of the sleeve. Secure it with clothes pegs while drying.

7. Add features and trimmings to complete the head.

Note: *A similar sleeve puppet with a moving mouth can be made with other objects instead of a paper plate. For example, an egg box, used widthways or sideways, or another hinged container would be suitable. It might be helpful to reinforce the hinge by gluing a piece of strong fabric along it.*

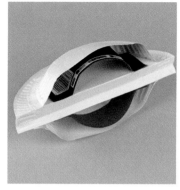

A second plate, cut in half, enhances the shape of the head.

Testing the mouth action before finishing the head.

The fabric sleeve is glued to the inside of the head and held with paper clips while setting.

A circle of felt is used to line the mouth but card, or even coloured paper, could be used.

With features added, the puppet is ready to use.

A cheesebox head

Materials: a cheesebox (the round, cardboard variety often used for triangles of cheese spread), matchbox or other small box, cardboard, trimmings.

1. Make two matching cuts into the sides of the lid and the bottom of the cheesebox so that the matchbox will just fit between the cuts.
2. Glue the matchbox into the bottom piece with half inside the box and half sticking out. This becomes the neck. Glue the two parts of the cheesebox back together.

3. Select trimmings and any padding required to give the head more shape. Padding is not essential but the back of the head of this puppet was padded with foam rubber before adding the hair.
4. Cut a piece of card to cover the face and neck and glue it in place before adding the features and hair.

Slits cut in the edge of the cheesebox head enable a matchbox to fit neatly as the neck.

These trimmings are ready to turn the cheesebox into a character.

The back of the head is padded to give it more shape.

Two-finger manipulation in the neck allows the head to turn without turning the puppet's body.

Although the face is flat, the addition of features gives it more depth.

An eggbox head

Materials: an eggbox.

1. Cut off the flap that normally secures the lid closed. Cut away sufficient to enable you to insert your fingers for manipulation.
2. Glue the edges of the box together and add features to whichever side you choose.

The flap on the eggbox is cut away to insert either two or four fingers, whatever is more comfortable for the performer.

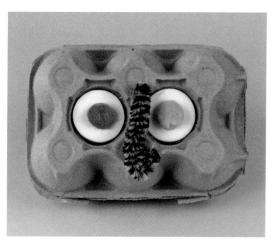

The eggbox head needed few features added to make it an owl.

A tin can head

Materials: tin can, cardboard tube, foam rubber, trimmings.

Tin cans often have a paper covering that can be removed, painted over or covered with paper or thin card, depending on the surface required and the features to be added. Cover any sharp edges with foam rubber, fabric or a few layers of masking tape.

1. Add features to the can. Cut down a cardboard tube that will fit fully into the can with sufficient protruding to form a neck.
2. Secure the tube in the can with glued pieces of foam squashed in between the can and the tube.

Tin cans often have paper covering that can be removed or kept as a base for attaching a suitable covering.

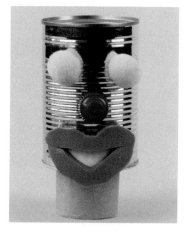

The neck tube is glued in place with foam padding and the sharp edge of the can is covered with layers of masking tape.

A carton head for an animal

Materials: plastic carton, cardboard, trimmings, newspaper.

Cartons and containers, upright, tilted or inverted, may immediately suggest human or animal heads or body shapes. Which way up they are used depends upon the type of puppet. This example uses a yoghurt pot for an animal head. It had a thick paper covering which was removed for the illustrations, but it is a good idea to retain it as it makes the carton stronger. Subsequent covering compensated for this.

1. Select a carton of suitable shape and size and a cardboard tube for the neck.
2. Make a hole a short distance from the edge of the carton to accommodate the neck.
3. Glue a little packing into the top of the cardboard tube. This will give a larger surface for gluing the tube in place.
4. Glue this end of the tube and glue around the hole in the carton, then push the neck securely in place.

5. It may help to use strong adhesive tape along the tube and inside the carton.
6. Glue the lid or a piece of card over the end of the carton before adding any covering and features.

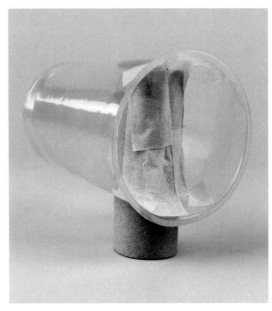

The cardboard tube for the neck needs to be firmly fixed in place.

A plastic yoghurt pot makes a good animal head. The neck is fixed for use as a glove puppet.

Simple coverings help to make the carton more durable.

A plastic bottle animal

Materials: a plastic bottle, coloured paper, a short, thick tube, trimmings.

1. With the bottle on its side, mark the edges of a slot to be cut to accommodate two fingers.
2. Cut out the slot and fold masking tape around the edges of the hole to protect the sharp edges.
3. Insert a piece of tubing into the hole and glue it just forward of the slot to take your fingers. In the example shown, a piece of tubular foam was used.
4. Glue a covering over the bottle and its neck. Here paper was used for the main body and a stretchy plastic tube was used for the neck with a short, thick cardboard tube wedged into the neck of the bottle.
5. Add trimmings and features.

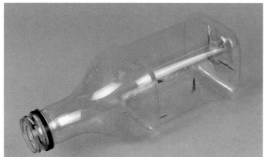

A bottle is marked ready for cutting away a rectangular section.

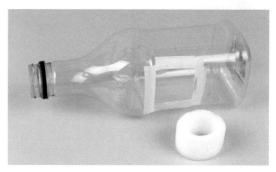

The sharp edges of the opening are covered with masking tape to protect the performer's fingers.

A short piece of foam tubing is glued inside the bottle to aid manipulation.

Two fingers are inserted into the bottle and the foam tubing to check the degree of control.

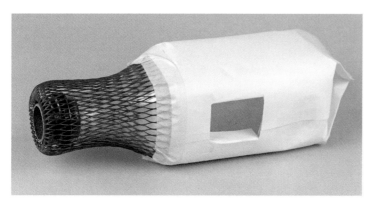

A paper covering and stretchy mesh tubing over the head.

Ribbon is stapled into loops to become ears.

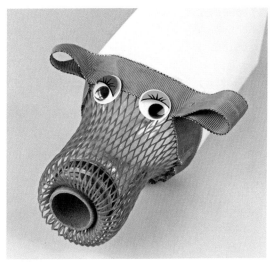

The ears and eyes are glued on and this could become a few different animals. The bottle neck could be a nose or a mouth.

A fabric puppet

The heads of fabric puppets are often made as part of the entire figure, as is the case with this fur fabric animal. The description of this puppet's construction is in Chapter 4.

This furry hand puppet can be given a mouth, tucked in like a sock puppet, or it can be used as a tube with the mouth 'implied'.

Rod Puppet Heads

A wooden spoon head

A wooden spoon needs only a few features added, or even painted on, to become a basic rod puppet head. Self-adhesive eyes, a fluffy ball nose and a pipe-cleaner mouth are combined with a feather for hair on this character.

Just a few features, without any face covering, create the head for a very simple rod puppet.

A paper plate head

Paper plates can be simply a face upon which the features are added. This lends itself well to rod puppets for which a draped costume or a full body can be added.

Features stuck onto the paper plate create a lively head that is more vibrant than a flat painted face.

A ball head

A ball with a hole in it is easily fixed onto a rod and glued or pinned in place with a drawing pin

This airflow ball is now used as a rod puppet, with or without any covering of the head.

through the top of the ball. The illustration shows an airflow ball which already has convenient holes for the control rod and a dowelling nose.

Another ball head

Materials: a ball, an old pair of thick tights, dowel rod, drawing pin, thread or tape.

1. Make a hole in the ball and insert a dowel rod of the required length. Secure the rod with a drawing pin through the top of the ball to stop it wobbling – unless you want it to wobble.
2. Cut one leg from an old pair of tights and insert the ball and the rod up into the toe.
3. Tie or tape around the neck securely.
4. Cut off any surplus from the tights, leaving sufficient to cover the body.

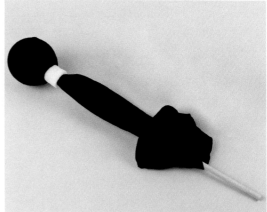

An old ball with a rod inserted forms the head of a rod puppet. The head is covered with a leg from a thick pair of tights.

A carton head

Materials: a carton or container of any shape or size, dowel rod, masking tape, nail or drawing pin, trimmings.

1. Secure a container to the top of a dowel rod; glue the top of the rod and further secure it with a nail or drawing pin pushed through the carton.
2. Wedge some tubing or foam rubber into any gap between the rod and the neck of the container to hold it firmly in place.
3. Add any trimmings and features.

A head for a table-top puppet

Table-top puppets may have the main control rod to the head through the body, as described for other rod puppets, but often this rod is connected directly to the head to facilitate greater head movement, as exemplified here.

Materials: a strong cardboard box, block of foam rubber, dowel rod, cord.

1. Having chosen a suitable box for the head, decide where you want to attach the control rod. This might conveniently be at the back of the head, a short distance above the neck.
2. With the lid off the box, make a hole just big enough for the dowel rod at this point and insert the rod at a slight upwards angle.
3. In the bottom edge of the box, make a hole for a cord to attach the neck.

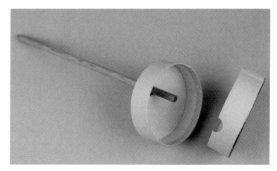

This head rod for a table-top puppet is the main control for the figure, but alternative control methods are possible.

Plastic cartons with inbuilt handles provide ready-made heads that are quickly adapted to rod puppets.

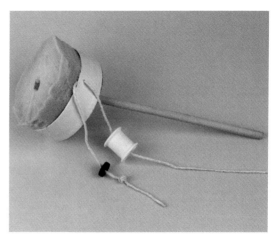

It is important to secure the attachment for the neck before sealing the head sections together.

4. Trim a block of foam rubber to fit snuggly inside the box and glue it in place with the rod withdrawn.
5. When the glue is dry, reinsert the dowel rod through the foam rubber. You might be able to simply push it through or make a guide hole with a sharp object. Glue the rod in place.
6. Glue the lid onto the box. If required, build out the head shape with suitable containers.
7. Add features and trimmings.

A sculpted foam rubber head
Materials: block of foam rubber.

1. Draw the full-face and profile views of the head on two sides of a block of foam rubber, making sure that the profile view is sufficiently deep; a common fault is to make the back of the head too square because the block was too shallow.
2. Cut away the main pieces of waste to establish the basic shape.

The back of the head is given more shape by a plastic container to which the hair will be added.

A head sculpted from a block of foam rubber; most of the shaping was completed with an old bread knife.

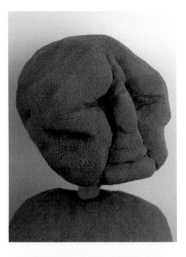

The features and hair now give the puppet a character.

This is a demonstration head, sculpted in foam rubber, with a moving mouth slotted at the back for hand operation, similar to a paper plate sleeve puppet.

3. Work on the detail, keeping the modelling quite bold. You can pull pieces of foam rubber off and/or glue foam rubber features onto the basic shape.
4. Add features as required.

Note: *See the earlier section 'Cutting' for advice on shaping foam rubber and, if you want to paint it, mix the paint very thickly and apply it to the surface of the foam rubber with your fingers, rubbing it in. If you apply the paint with a brush, it is likely to sink in and will remain wet for a long time.*

Marionette Heads

Many of the methods for making heads for different types of puppet are interchangeable. For a marionette, consider how you will make the neck joint, which is described in Chapter 3, and ensure the head is sufficiently sturdy to support the weight when head strings and the rest of the puppet are attached.

A ball head for a marionette

Materials: an old ball, a leg from thick tights, a dowel rod, thread or cord.

1. Cut one leg from an old pair of tights and insert the ball into the toe.
2. Gather up the material around the ball and tie a piece of thread or cord around it for the puppet's neck.
3. Cut off any surplus from the tights, leaving sufficient to make the joint to the body.

A carton head

A wide variety of cartons can be used for marionette heads. One example is a sturdy container that could be used for quite a large figure. It is covered with white card that helps the features to show up and provides a good surface on which to glue them.

The other example is for a smaller figure but the head itself does not take any weight. The head strings and the neck are attached to a wire fixed across the head as shown in Chapter 3, Bodies, Limbs and Joints.

When using large cartons for a head, be aware that a body and limbs of corresponding size can become extremely heavy to operate, so select materials accordingly.

Thin, flexible cartons need secure fixings, usually built into the head, for attaching head strings and making the neck joint.

A ball, secured in a toe cut from tights, provides the basis for a marionette head with a flexible neck.

A polystyrene egg head

Materials: egg-shaped polystyrene, trimmings.

Polystyrene egg shapes are popular for head shapes as only a tilt of the angle changes it from a human to an animal appearance. This example needs little change for it to become a snake; all it needs are the joints for attaching the body and the addition of simple features.

Polystyrene eggs offer a basis for both human and animal characters provided they have a secure means for making the attachments to neck and body.

A head from wooden off-cuts

Exploring off-cuts of wood can provide inspiration for puppet heads. Grouping and re-grouping the wooden pieces may suggest a variety of possibilities. This example used five blocks with angled ends.

These corner blocks from a large wooden frame were explored to see what they could become.

1. Glue together three of the blocks in different orientations to suggest a head. Keep the fourth block aside to be used as the shoulders.
2. Glue on other wooden off-cuts for the features.

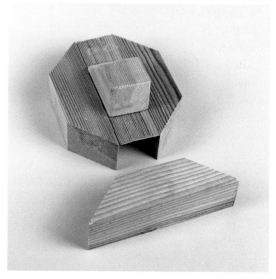

Three longer blocks and a short one form the head while a longer one suggests shoulders.

The head assembled with the neck attached.

FINISHING TOUCHES

Features

Some of the puppet's features may be integral to the shape of the object chosen for the head, but usually extra features need to be added. Sometimes all that is required to establish a face or a character is a single feature; the audience supplies the rest with their imagination.

Additional features can be painted onto the head if the surface is suitable, but this can look rather flat compared with colourful, three-dimensional features created from anything to hand that fits your purpose. The features on the heads in this chapter provide examples of more than twenty different objects or materials, including curled card, bottle tops, trimmed carton lids, buttons, beads, fur, coloured pipe cleaners, fluffy balls, ribbon, shaped and folded cardboard, self-adhesive spots, parts of old costume jewellery and even a walnut shell.

Eyes are often shiny so that they reflect the light, which gives them more life, but they can be made from anything you want to use. If you need to liven up the eyes, a quick dab of varnish or slightly diluted PVA glue may do the trick.

Adding wooden eyes

Moving wooden eyes were introduced for one of the puppets, as described below. With the eyes suspended on threads, this was more of a fun feature than a controlled movement.

Materials: plastic carton head, pre-drilled wooden balls, paper clips, strong thread.

1. Open a paper clip into a 'U' shape and insert the ends through the hole in the ball. Leave a little of the looped end protruding. Do this for both balls.
2. Bend the ends tight against the balls to secure them and cut off the excess wire.

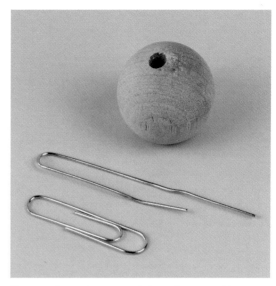

Stage one in creating suspended wooden eyes, with pre-drilled balls and an opened-up paper clip.

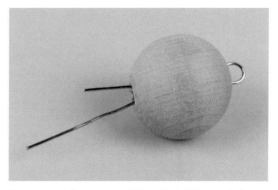

The paper clip is pressed right into the ball, leaving just enough of the loop to attach a thread.

Excess lengths of the paper clips are cut away and the ends are pressed closely against the ball.

3. Make small holes in the carton where you intend to suspend the eyes and cut open a flap at the back of the carton to provide access.
4. Insert strong thread through the wire loops and through the holes in the carton to suspend the eyes.
5. Tie the ends together with the eyes hanging at any length you choose. In the example shown, the eyes are for a rod puppet, so the thread is conveniently tied around the central rod.
6. Close and seal the back flap.

The back of the head is cut open to enable the wooden eyes to be secured.

The suspended eyeballs are secured. Are eye details needed or are they sufficient just as they are?

Hair

Puppeteers often use wools, string (thick and rough, or thin, smooth parcel string), fur, feathers, embroidery threads, brush bristles, sisal fibre (used to make rope or twine), goat hair and horsehair for their puppets' hair. Any of these items would be suitable for instant puppets but you might also use pipe cleaners, curled paper or card, or even coloured tissue paper.

If you decide to include eyebrows, you can use any material you want, but it is helpful to know that light-coloured eyebrows do not carry well to an audience, so puppeteers tend to use darker colours even when the hair is a light colour.

To create hair from a ball of wool or cord, wind it around a suitably sized piece of cardboard. Tie the loops together and then cut through them wherever you want. Cutting at the end opposite the knot will provide hair of equal length all round. Cutting on one side of the loop nearer the knot will produce the equivalent of long hair with a fringe.

Layers of tissue paper in different colours serve well as hair for this finger puppet.

Feathers can be used for hair, but this is an unusual way that seems to suit this puppet.

Dark eyebrows help to emphasise the eyes, even with light-colour hair where the same colour eyebrows would have a weaker effect.

Winding wool or other materials around stiff card is a quick way to prepare hair. Where it is tied and where it is cut will affect how it looks and the styles possible.

It is not essential to cut though the loops of wool; it depends on the look you want to achieve.

COSTUMES

Instant puppets sometimes have no costume at all, but it is assumed that any costume would need to be quickly assembled, for which a variety of methods is described.

Materials

Soft fabrics tend to move well whereas stiff or thick fabrics restrict movement, though they are useful for trimming. Thin fabrics let light shine through, and large prints do not suit small puppets. When selecting a fabric, see how it hangs on the straight and on the cross; jersey fabric cut on the cross is particularly suitable for flowing robes.

Try combining or overlaying fabrics of different colour, texture, or transparency to achieve variety; puppets dressed in only one fabric may not look so interesting. Try different shades of the same colour or combining contrasting colours. For trimmings, use fringing, braids, ribbons, lace, faux fur, feathers, beads, costume jewellery, felt and so on.

For speed, glove puppets are quickly made with material draped over your hand rather than the standard 'glove' body which takes longer to make and achieve a comfortable fit. However, if a glove is required as a basis for adding a costume or trimmings, instructions are included in Chapter 4, Hand Puppets. It might be useful to create a few glove bodies with elasticated necks for use with different heads and different costumes.

Children's clothes that are no longer needed often provide suitable puppet costumes, especially for rod puppets and marionettes, and they will save a considerable amount of time.

Note: *For a marionette, you need to dress the puppet before attaching the strings. Sometimes you might need to secure the hands and feet after adding sleeves and trouser legs, depending how the costume is made and the size of the hands and feet.*

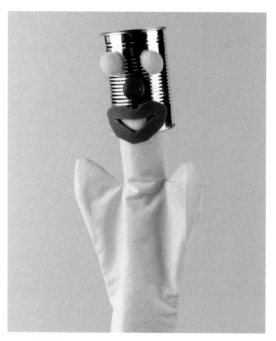

A standard 'glove' body provides an excellent base upon which to create a costume.

Clothes that children have outgrown are a good source of costumes for instant puppets.

Draped Costumes

Lengths of fabric draped around the figure can make an effective costume. This allows the natural movement of the fabric to enhance the puppet's movements. Attaching a piece of fabric in this way, without spoiling it, is economical, enabling it to be used for different purposes on different occasions. If necessary, it can be held in place by an occasional stitch, a spot of glue, an elastic band, a safety pin, or adhesive tape.

Sewing a Costume

Sewing a costume is not normally needed for instant puppets but it is possible if you have the skill. You can make up the costume by stitching it together by hand or by machine but be careful not to make it too tight. A good alternative is to stitch the costume together by hand directly on the puppet. The alternative methods described here tend to be much quicker and are popular for instant puppets.

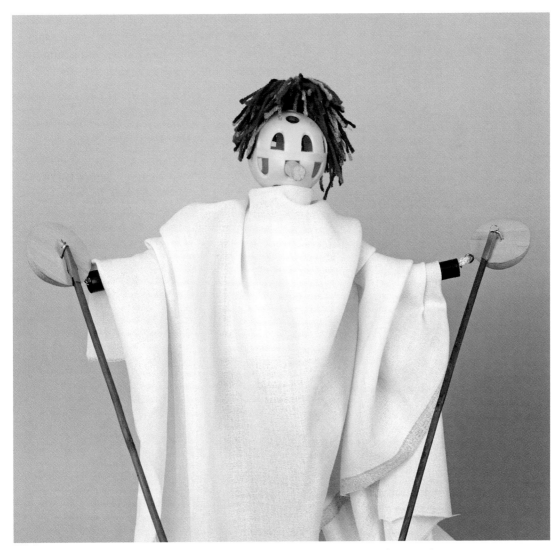

Draping fabric onto the puppet without cutting holes in it keeps open the possibility of re-using the fabric for other puppetry projects.

Gluing a Costume

Gluing is much quicker than sewing and leaves no seam edges inside the clothes to hinder movement.

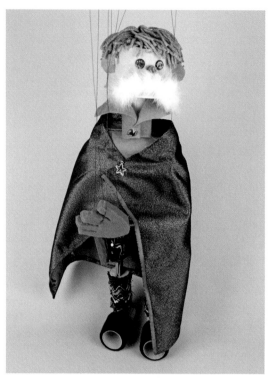

The costume was glued to this puppet, using pieces of fabric that would have been too small to make into an entire garment.

1. To make a hem, smear glue sparingly but evenly along the edge, turn it up and press down firmly.

2. To make a seam, glue one edge and press it on top of the other; the glue prevents the outer edge fraying. Use this method to make tubes of fabric for sleeves and trouser legs.

3. For a shirt or a jacket, begin with the front and back panels. A shirt under a jacket needs only a strip of material down the front of the body and a narrower strip for the collar.

4. Add the sleeve tubes, cut at an angle at the top so that they fit neatly onto the costume at the shoulders.

5. For trouser legs, make tubes in the same way as the sleeves but smear glue along the overlapping edge up as far as the crotch and snip a little into both edges of the fabric at the crotch so that the fabric can be opened out at the top to meet the matching fabric from the other leg.

6. With the trouser legs on the puppet, glue together the fly front, under the crotch and up the back of the trousers. To make a waistband, glue a strip of material into a narrow tube shape. Press it flat with the join inside and glue it over the join between the trousers and the shirt.

7. Add the shirt collar and any other trimmings to complete the costume.

8. The shoes are covered with faux leather as shown in Chapter 3.

The quickest way of making a hem and preventing fraying is with a single line of glue and a turned edge of the fabric.

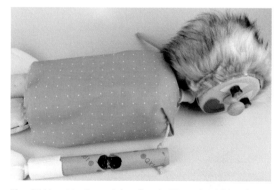

The shirt is cut to size and then fitted with a snip and a tuck wherever needed. Back and front panels are attached separately.

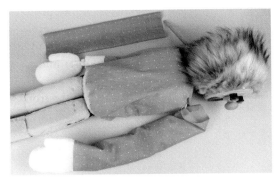

Lengths of fabric made into tubes become the sleeves. They might need attaching before the large hands, or it will help if the hands are detachable until dressing is complete.

Both sleeves are finished and neatly attached to the shoulders.

Larger tubes of fabric for the legs are left open at the top for joining up the front, back and crotch.

With the trousers finished, a waistband covers the join with the shirt.

Dresses usually require front and back panels for the bodice, with sleeves added. The skirt may be cut in one piece or in a few panels. However, you can achieve very effective dresses by draping the fabric and stitching or gluing it in place rather than making up an actual dress.

To complete the costume, a collar is added and the tops of the shoes are covered with faux leather.

CHAPTER 3

BODIES, LIMBS AND JOINTS

People and animals come in all manner of shapes and sizes and, fortunately, cartons and containers do too, so there will be no shortage of different items to suit the characters you want to make. Please remember the advice in the previous chapter to think about the whole puppet when you are designing it, so that you have a good idea of how the different parts will join together, even though you may make adjustments as construction progresses.

THE BODY AND WAIST JOINTS

The body of most puppets is the core to which all other parts are joined, so ensure that it is sufficiently strong to accept any attachments that will remain secure when performing.

Hand Puppets

Glove puppets
Glove puppets frequently have the traditional 'glove' shape that forms the body, the arms and hands, the construction of which is described in Chapter 4. The puppeteer's wrist acts as the waist of a glove puppet so it is advisable to make the glove long enough to reach the elbow so that the performer's arm does not show when the puppet bends forward.

It is not easy for young children to make gloves that are a good fit and comfortable to manipulate, so other types of puppet might be more suitable. However, if they are to have glove puppets, it may be useful to have sets of ready-made gloves in different sizes with elasticated or draw-thread necks, ready to be used without delay with any head and a draped costume.

Sleeve puppets
Sleeve puppets depend upon the performer's arm for their body, but a body shape may be added by padding attached to the puppeteer's wrist inside the costume. A small sleeve puppet may have a waist in the same way as a glove puppet, but larger figures usually do not appear below waist level.

A hand puppet glove ready for any head and costume.

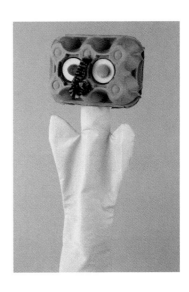

OPPOSITE: The performer's arm is a sleeve puppet's body. It is also called a mouth puppet, for obvious reasons.

Carton bodies

A plastic container may serve as both the head and body of a hand puppet and is particularly useful for animal characters, as described in Chapter 4, Hand Puppets.

The bottle converted to an animal.

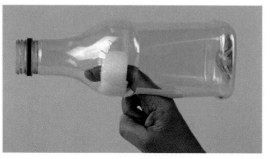

A plastic bottle as a basis for an animal puppet.

Rod Puppets

An improvised body

A simple body shape, like a wooden-spoon rod puppet, may have a body added but this can be achieved simply by extending the thumb and index finger of the hand holding the spoon.

Carton bodies

Rod puppets with a long central control rod may have their entire body shape suggested by the shape of a carton and they do not bend at the waist. Those with shorter rods can bend at the waist; they may have a shorter container for the torso, with the puppeteer's wrist acting as the waist.

The performer's outstretched thumb and fingers give the costume shape.

Components of a rod puppet with a carton body.

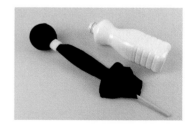

Puppets with shorter cartons and rods can bend at the waist.

Shoulder blocks

Often rod puppets have just a shoulder block to establish a body shape and to provide attachments for arms and costume. It may be fixed securely to the rod and the head or supported in place so that the head can turn independently of the body, which is the preferred method.

To achieve this:

1. Cut a hole through the shoulder block sufficient to allow it to turn freely on the central rod without being loose and wobbly.

2. Secure it in place by attaching to the rod some form of 'collar' which will prevent the shoulders slipping down but allow them to turn. The collar may be a strip of cardboard glued to, and wound around, the rod; alternatively, use strong adhesive tape, or a block of foam rubber.

3. To prevent the shoulders sticking on the collar, it is a good idea to cut one or two circles from plastic lids to act as washers between the shoulders and the collar.

A selection of cartons and lids used as shoulder blocks.

A disc cut from a plastic lid serves as a washer between the shoulders and the supporting collar.

The supporting collar is glued to the rod close to the shoulders.

Animal rod puppets

Hand puppet and rod puppet animals are often made with upright bodies, but for a typical rod puppet a strong cardboard tube is a good basis for the body as it provides secure attachments for the control rods. A rod puppet made this way will often need two rods; one to support and turn the head and one to support the body.

Interchangeable bodies

Similar items can be used for rod puppet and marionette bodies, the main difference being whether the head and body are attached to each other by a rod or by a joint that allows greater flexibility for a marionette. Otherwise, the principles for attaching limbs are similar.

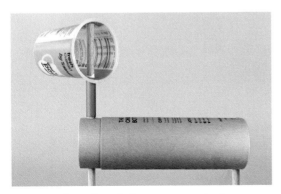
A carton and a cardboard tube suggest an animal.

These cartons can form the basis of a rod puppet or a marionette.

Flexible bodies

Puppets with flexible bodies provide the option of making them as marionettes or as rod puppets that may be operated from below or from above, as described in Chapter 5. Often, the body has a central core of cord which allows considerable flexibility and is easily threaded through the body parts. A core of flexible tubing requires larger holes through the separate sections, so it is not suitable for some bodies.

The separate body segments may be any ball, discs or blocks in a wide range of materials. It is helpful if the items chosen already have holes through the centre or if holes can easily be made with a suitable tool or needle. Materials that are not spherical move better if small balls or beads are threaded between each segment.

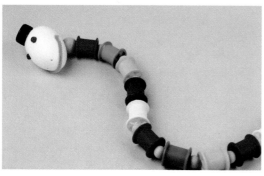

Beads between each body segment help the flexibility of this colourful animal.

An embroidery needle was used to pierce ping-pong balls and thread them on a cord.

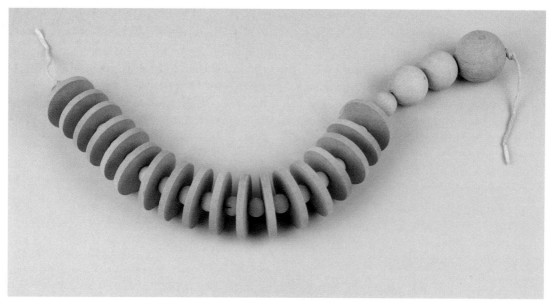

Pre-drilled wooden discs and small balls give the puppet weight that aids manipulation.

Marionettes

Carton bodies

Plastic cartons are excellent for ready-made marionette bodies.

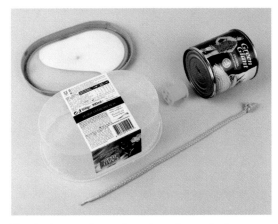

The plastic carton is a ready-made marionette body.

Marionette bodies can also be constructed quite quickly from cartons or spare materials. At a very basic level, cardboard tubes can be joined together by cord.

1. Pierce holes through each of the cardboard tubes about 2cm or 3cm from each end.
2. Thread the cord through the holes and knot each end with two or three knots so that they cannot pull through the tube. Ensure that the cords on the left- and right-hand sides are of equal length. The distance between the top and bottom knot determines the flexibility of the body.
3. Glue the knots to seal them and glue around the holes to strengthen them.

Cardboard tubes linked together with cord to form a body.

Bodies built on a central core

A more substantial marionette body can be constructed using a leather, faux leather or fabric central core sandwiched between blocks of foam rubber, balsa wood or other available material shaped as required for the character. This method permits bending but prevents turning at the waist.

1. Make templates for the body sections from strong card.
2. Punch three holes in the card, not too close to the edge, to provide fixing points for neck and shoulders.
3. Use the templates to draw and cut out the central core, allowing a suitable gap for the waist and an extension at the bottom for attaching the legs.
4. Use the cardboard templates to draw the body shapes on the blocks that will provide the bulk of the body.

A strip of faux leather is the core, waist and hip joints for a marionette.

Cardboard templates are used to draw the outline on the padding for the body.

5. Trim the body to shape. To facilitate bending, cut away a wedge between the front blocks at the waist.

Note: If you use foam rubber blocks for the body, please note the advice on shaping it described in the previous chapter.

6. Before joining all the parts together, make the attachments required for the neck and arms on the cardboard templates. Often these will be strong cord but other options are possible, as outlined later in this chapter.

7. Glue the templates and the shaped blocks together on the central core. While drying, it is helpful to hold the separate sections in place by wrapping a little masking tape around the top and bottom segments.

The foam rubber blocks were lightly trimmed to shape with scissors and glued to the cardboard templates which are themselves glued to the central core.

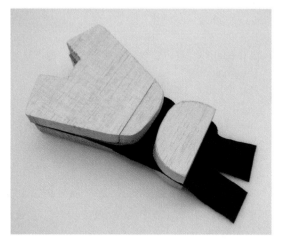

Balsa wood blocks used for shaping the body.

A waist joint with greater flexibility

1. Omit the central faux leather core that serves as the waist and hip joints and link the cardboard templates with strong, knotted cord that is threaded through a ball to give smooth bending and turning at the waist.

2. Use the templates to outline the padding for the body and trim it to shape as described above.

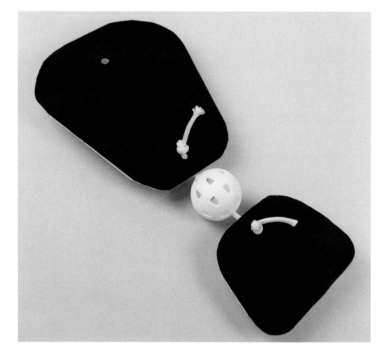

A cord through a plastic ball provides a very flexible waist joint.

NECK JOINTS

Hand Puppet Neck Joints

Hand puppets normally have the puppeteer's hand or fingers inserted directly into the neck or head so there is no actual neck joint, except for a glove puppet which has the neck of the fabric glove attached to the neck built into the head.

- If the fabric neck is elasticated, pull it onto the neck of the puppet.
- If it has a draw-thread, put it in place and tighten the thread; tie the knot with a bow so that it can be removed easily.
- For an alternative, temporary method, use double-sided tape between the neck and the fabric.
- For a permanent joint, glue the fabric on to the neck.

Rod Puppet Neck Joints

Rod puppets are best constructed so that the head is not loose and does not wobble on the main control rod.

- If the neck of the chosen carton is wider than the rod it sits on, insert packing such as paper, card or foam rubber between the neck and the rod to achieve a tight fit.
- If the rod reaches the top of the head, put adhesive on the tip and secure it further with a nail, screw or drawing pin down through the top of the head.

These methods, with a supported shoulder block described above, enable the head to turn.

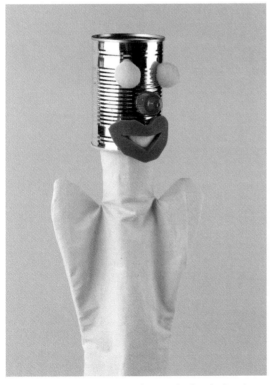

The neck of the glove body can be attached to the head permanently or temporarily, so it can be used with other heads.

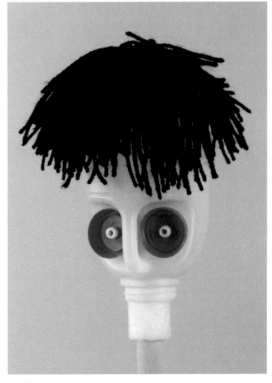

Packing around the rod gives a tight fit for a loose neck.

A pivoted head

If the head is to nod or look up, pivot the head on the central rod or a strong tube.

1. Insert a stiff piece of wire, such as coat-hanger wire, across the head from side to side and through holes made or drilled in the tube or rod. Try to judge the best point of balance for inserting the wire across the head. This can be a little tricky but, if the head is to be decorated, it will not hurt to make a few test holes which will then be covered up.
2. Use tubing, beads, or any suitable material that will not grip, as spacers on the wire to keep the rod central on the head.
3. If the head moves too far up or down, glue or tape foam rubber, or other padding, inside the head at the front and/or the back to limit its range of movement.
3. When the movement is satisfactory, bend the ends of the wire over to stop it coming out. These ends may be hidden by the ears when the head is decorated.

A head pivoted on a tube needs spacers to keep the tube centralised.

Marionette Neck Joints

Marionettes are generally required to have a good range of head movement so a flexible joint at the neck is desirable. The joint should be strong and secure as the head and shoulders together support the weight of the entire body and limbs.

The pivoted head for a rod puppet works well for marionettes and the neck can be joined to the body in such a way that allows turning as well as nodding.

Hollow cans and containers enable a variety of neck joints that allow the head to twist and turn in any direction. Select suitable items for the head, neck, and body. It will help if the neck already has a hole through the centre; if it does not, try to select something in which a hole can be made easily, rather than something that requires drilling.

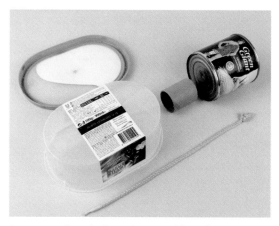

A strong cardboard tube makes a suitable neck.

Cord joints

1. Make a central hole in the bottom of the head and another in the top of the body.
2. Knot one end of a strong cord with large knots and thread the other end down through the hole in the head, neck and body.
3. Knot the cord inside the body; although it should not be too loose, avoid making it too tight or it may limit the range of movement.

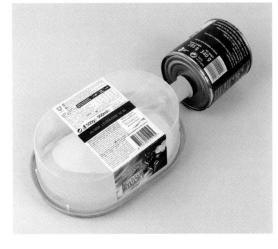

Knotted cord inside the head and body secures the cotton-reel neck.

Sometimes it is not easy to access the inside of the containers to tie the knots but there are alternatives for making this joint. A container with a screw-on lid can be used if inverted for the head.

1. Knot the end of the joining cord and thread it through a bead or any small object that will prevent it pulling through the joint.
2. Thread the cord up through a hole in the centre of the body, through the neck and through a hole made in the centre of the lid.
3. Knot the cord securely inside the lid and screw the lid back on to the container.

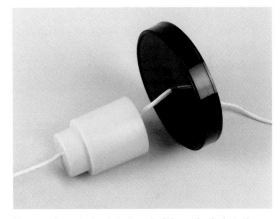

The cord from the body is threaded through a hole in the centre of the neck and another in the lid of the carton, then knotted securely.

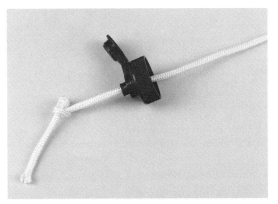

The cord is knotted below a bottle top before it is inserted inside the body. The cord is threaded through a hole in the top of the box, ready to make the neck joint.

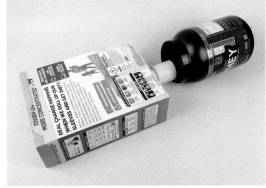

The lid is screwed firmly back onto the carton to complete the joint between head and body.

Alternative joints

A treasury tag is a quick and easy way to make a neck joint if you can find a tag of a suitable length, or if you adjust the length of the neck to fit the tag.

1. Make a small hole in the centre of the base of the head and in the top-centre of the body.
2. Insert the ends of the treasury tag through the neck and through these holes to make the joint.
3. If the joint needs to be quite tight, make the joint initially without the neck, split the neck along its length and insert it over the cord between head and body.

A similar method is useful for joints with narrow-necked plastic bottles.

1. Use a large needle to thread a cord through the centre of a small ball, such as a ping-pong ball.
2. Tie each end of the cord to a short piece of dowelling.
3. Glue the knots and glue them to the centre of the dowels.
4. When dry, insert one dowel through a hole made in the base of the head and insert the other dowel into the neck of the bottle. When it is fully inside the bottle, it will twist around and prevent it coming out.

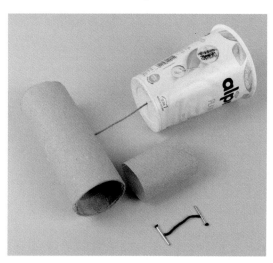

A treasury tag is used for a simple neck joint.

A cord through a ball is tied and glued to short dowels to make the neck joint.

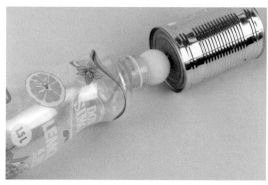

The dowels are inserted into the head and fully into the bottle neck to secure the joint.

For a tight joint, split the neck tube open, put it over the tag, and glue it back together.

Necks and joints for nodding and turning heads

There is a variety of ways to create a controlled nodding and turning action, the first of which is similar to the nodding rod puppet described above.

1. Pivot the head on a hollow neck by a wire with spacers used to keep the neck central within the head.
2. Thread strong cord through a hole made in the top-centre section of the body.
3. Pull the cord through far enough to knot the end securely, smear it with glue and pull it back fully inside the body.
4. Knot the cord again on top of the body and thread the end up through a ball on which the neck will roll.
5. Knot the cord securely on top of the ball, glue the knot and glue the ball into the bottom of the neck.

If you use a ball and tube of suitable dimensions, they will be a tight, secure fit. Otherwise, it will be necessary to insert short tacks into the ball through the tube to secure the joint.

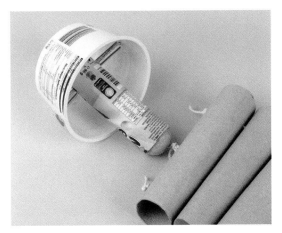

The neck tube is pivoted for nodding and the ball at the base enables turning and rolling in any direction.

Dowelling necks and joints

Dowel rods of suitable diameter provide a variety of options for nodding and turning heads, using screw-eyes in the ends or holes drilled across the dowel to accommodate cords or lengths of coat-hanger wire for fastening in the head and the body. Those using cords will allow greater flexibility while those using wires will restrict movement in certain directions if this is required.

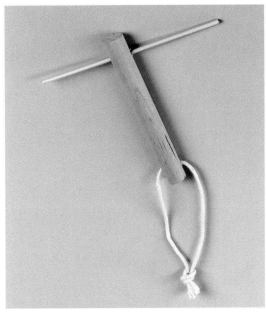

The wire may be used to secure a dowel in the head while the cord provides a flexible attachment to the body.

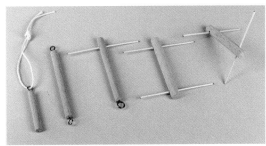

These different neck arrangements offer a variety of options for limiting or enabling head movement.

Wooden off-cuts

A head made of wooden off-cuts, like the one illustrated, may be linked to the body by a tubular neck.

1. Insert a suitable screw-eye into the back of the head and thread a strong cord through it.
2. Thread both ends of the cord down through the tube chosen for the neck.
3. Continue to thread the cord through a hole drilled in the shoulder section of the body and knot the ends with a series of large knots.

4. If there is any danger of the knot pulling back through the hole in the shoulders, undo the knot and thread one end of the cord through a bead before redoing the knot.
5. For each method, seal the knot with glue.

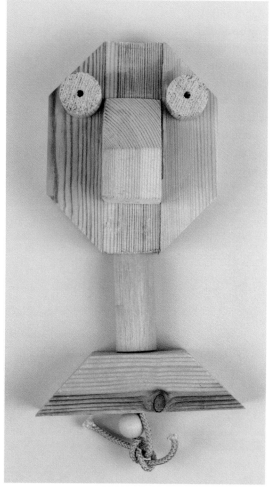

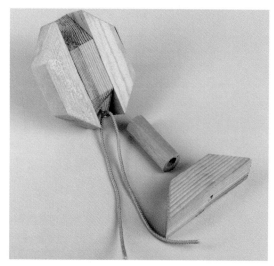

A pre-drilled wooden dowel was a happy discovery for this neck, but any tube will serve the purpose.

Tie the knot around a bead or ball for extra security.

Ensure the knotted cord cannot pull back through the hole in the shoulders.

ARMS AND ELBOW JOINTS

Hand Puppets

Glove puppets normally have no arms. Instead, the glove body has short arms/hands with bending movement restricted to the puppeteer's fingers and thumb. A separate wrist and hand may be added, as described below in the section on hands.

Large sleeve puppets may have a long 'glove' as part of the costume to fit on the hand and arm of the puppeteer. During use, care must be taken to keep the arm relatively close to the main figure. If necessary, it may be linked to the puppet by fabric tape or cord to prevent the arm straying away.

The performer has a costumed hand and arm for this sleeve puppet.

Rod Puppets and Marionettes

The materials and joints used for the arms and elbows of rod puppets or marionettes are largely interchangeable with those used for legs and knees, differing mainly in length, bulk and the degree of flexibility required. Legs tend to need somewhat more restricted lateral movement for a good walking action while arms are required to be spread widely, to reach across the body and allow the hands to reach the head or face.

Rope arms

Arms made entirely of rope, or of tubes threaded on rope or cord, offer considerable scope for movement.

To improve smooth movement between tubes at the elbow, thread a bead or a wooden ball onto the cord at the elbow. If necessary, reduce the length of the tubing accordingly or the hands might hang too low.

An arm made entirely of rope.

Tubular arm sections on a central cord.

Beads or balls between the arm sections facilitate smooth movement.

Bottle arms

If tubing does not provide the required bulk for the arms, plastic bottles can serve the purpose.

1. Pierce a hole in the bottom of each bottle.
2. Thread the cord through the bottles, using a long 'needle' made from coat-hanger wire, as described in Chapter 2.
3. It will help movement if the bottles are positioned with the necks facing each other at the elbow joint.

For greater flexibility, use a bottle for the lower arm but leave the upper arm only as cord.

Plastic bottles used to give more bulk to the arms.

Foam rubber arms

Foam rubber and cord arms provide bulk and flexibility.

1. Cut lengths of foam rubber for each arm section and trim them to shape.
2. Using a long needle, thread the cord lengthways through the centre of each section, leaving sufficient space between them for the elbow to bend.
3. Add a spot of glue to the ends of each section to prevent them slipping down the cord.

Foam rubber arms provide bulk, and they can be trimmed to shape.

Dowelling arms

Short pieces of dowelling or sections from an old broom handle provide ready-made arms that need only the elbow joint, which can be made with screw-eyes.

Method 1

1. Screw a screw-eye into the end of each dowel. It is a good idea to make a small pilot hole first as this helps to avoid the dowel splitting.
2. Thread a piece of cord through both screw-eyes and tie the ends together.
3. Seal the knot with glue.

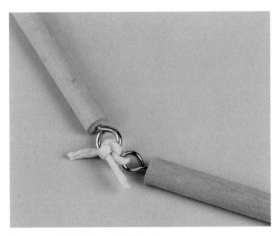

Screw-eyes linked by cord at the elbow.

Method 2

1. Open the loop of one screw-eye with pliers.
2. Hook it into another screw-eye and close the loop.
3. Screw the interlocked screw-eyes into the ends of the parts that are to be joined.

Interlocked screw-eyes for the elbow joint.

For an alternative to screw-eyes, using only cord:

1. Drill holes across each dowel, near the elbow.
2. Thread the cord through the holes and tie the ends together.

Holes drilled across the arm sections to take the cord that secures the elbow joint.

Cardboard tube arms

A similar cord joint that does not require drilling can be made with cardboard tubes.

1. Pierce holes through the sides of each tube, near but not too close to the edges.
2. Thread a piece of cord through the holes in each tube, tie the ends of the cord together and seal the knot with glue.

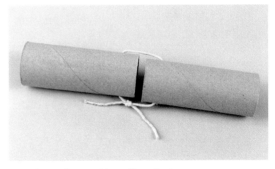

A similar cord joint with cardboard tubes.

For better elbow movement, cut a wedge shape in the tubes before proceeding to make the joint.

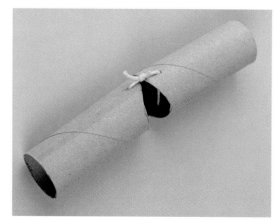

The arm sections are cut away in a wedge shape to improve the movement of the joint.

A strap joint

A strap joint can be used if you need to restrict elbow movement.

To make a simple restricted joint for cardboard tubes:

1. Join the two arm sections together using strong adhesive tape or fabric glued into each section.
2. If access is possible, staple through the strap and the tube for extra stability.

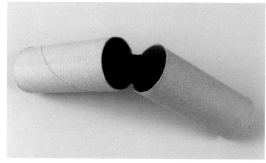

Strong adhesive tape makes a quick joint in cardboard tubes.

Thick tubing may require a different approach:

1. Cut a wedge shape from the tubes at the elbow.
2. Insert some packing into the cut-away section to produce a flat surface within the curved tube. In the example shown, off-cuts of a type of foam have been used.
3. Join the two arm sections together using strong adhesive tape or fabric glued into each section.

Thick tubes need some internal packing before using tape for the joint.

A restricted joint in foam rubber

You can trim foam rubber arms to shape before or after making this joint.

1. Cut a slot across each foam rubber block at the elbow, aligning the slots. The depth of the slot depends on the length of the arms but about 5cm is desirable.
2. Cut a wedge shape from each section at the elbow.
3. Cut a strap of faux leather or strong fabric the same length as the two slots together and a little wider than the arm sections.

4. Slot the strap into the slots to test the fit. The two sections should touch without any gap; if they do not, slightly shorten the strap or lengthen the slots accordingly.
5. Glue both sides of the strap, taking care not to glue the mid-point where it will bend, and slide the strap into each of the leg sections.
6. When the glue has set, trim away the spare pieces of strap at each side.
7. For extra security, glue and insert pins at an angle through the foam rubber and the strap.

Faux leather was used for this joint. The foam rubber can be trimmed to shape before or after making the joint.

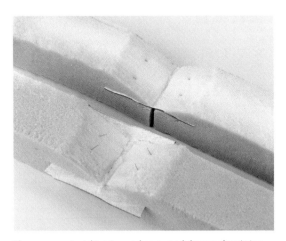

The spare material is trimmed away and dressmakers' pins can be used to help secure the joint.

Rope arms pass through the tubing of the body and the rope is glued in place.

SHOULDER JOINTS

For the arms described above, there are various ways to make the shoulder joint.

Arms with a Central Cord

One long cord can serve both arms. This offers three possibilities:

- Glue or tape the centre of the cord along the top of the body or shoulder block.

Cord through each arm is glued to the top of the shoulder block.

- Thread the cord through the body or shoulder sections. Glue or tape it down to keep the arms of equal length.

Leave sufficient space on the cord for flexibility of the arms.

- Thick rope arms may be secured by gluing small pieces of dowelling through them on either side of the body.

Dowelling used to secure the position of a thick rope.

Arms with Separate Central Cords

Insert the top of the cord through a hole in the body at the shoulder and knot the end of the cord. If the body is a soft material, such as foam rubber, thread the cord through strong card or a piece of a plastic container before tying the knot.

Securing a shoulder joint with a foam rubber shoulder block.

Other types of arm

Arms with no central cord may be attached to holes made in the body at the shoulder.

1. Tie one end of a piece of cord to the top of the arm. Either run the cord through holes across the top of the arm or tie it to screw-eyes in the top of a wooden arm.
2. Tie the other end of the cord through holes made in the body section or shoulder block.

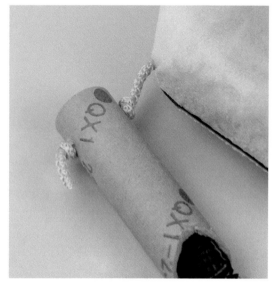

The cord is tied to the central core of the body, under the foam rubber padding.

HANDS AND WRIST JOINTS

Hand puppets

Sleeve puppets usually have a fabric hand and arm worn by the puppeteer, as described above for arms.

Glove puppets often do not have large shaped hands but they can have them as extensions to the traditional glove, if required. They can be cut from any material, but it is better if they are reasonably light so cutting them from card or foam rubber are good options.

1. Cut the hands in the chosen material, leaving sufficient at the wrist to make the joint.

2. To give the fingers an interesting position, glue and insert a fine wire into the fingers and use this to shape them.

3. Choose an existing cardboard tube or glue and tape a piece of card into a tube that will fit snuggly over the glove puppet's hands.

4. Glue the wrist of the hand securely into the end of the tube.

5. Insert the tube onto the glove puppet hand to ensure it is a good fit and then glue it in place.

6. When the costume is added to the basic glove, this will cover the cardboard tube. If it is glued to the tube, it will add to the security of the extended hands.

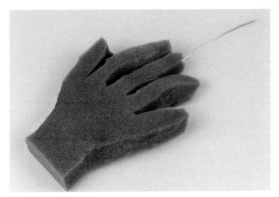

Wire is inserted into the foam rubber fingers to bend them into interesting shapes.

The hand is glued securely into the tube.

The tube containing the hand is added to a glove puppet.

Rod Puppets and Marionettes

Cardboard, foam rubber and wooden shapes lend themselves well to hands for rod puppets and marionettes. Alternatively, other objects that may not be realistic hand shapes may be used to represent hands.

You can make the hands any size you want, and you may enlarge or reduce them for effect, but it might be helpful to know that human hands are approximately the size from the chin to the middle of the forehead.

A cardboard hand is joined by knotted cord.

Cardboard hands

Cardboard hands may be attached to cord arms or to the central cord of tube or bottle arms.

1. Draw and cut out the hands in reasonably stiff cardboard.
2. Make a hole in the hand near the wrist.
3. Thread the cord through the hole and knot the end.
4. Glue the edge of the cord against the hand to keep it flat.
5. It helps if you can staple the card to the hand as well.

The cord is stapled to the card to help control the hand.

Foam rubber hands

Some types of foam, like that used in furnishings, may be shaped into hands. The plastic foam products of the type often used for packing and transporting televisions and computers tend to be much more difficult to cut and shape. These are best used for broadly shaped hands rather than those with finer detail.

Select any of the wrist joints detailed below for three-dimensional hands.

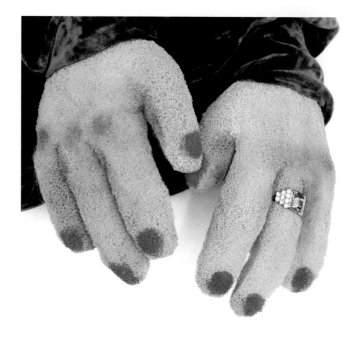

Foam rubber hands trimmed smooth and painted.

Wooden hands
Shaped wooden hands

Spare pieces of wood can be shaped into hands if you have a vice (preferably with wooden jaws), a saw and suitable rasps. The illustration shows three stages of shaping a hand.

1. Use a saw to cut the basic shape and refine the hard corners with a rasp.
2. Use a rasp to give more shape to the back of the hand so that it is not stiff and flat.
3. Continue to refine the shape by softening the edges more.

4. Detail may be achieved, if required, by adding grooves between fingers with a file but it is just as effective to paint the detail on the hands.
5. Insert a screw-eye into the edge of the hand to make the wrist joint.
6. Tie the screw-eye to a cord within the arm.

Alternatively, if the forearm is made of wood, use interlocked screw-eyes or screw-eyes tied together, as described previously for elbow joints.

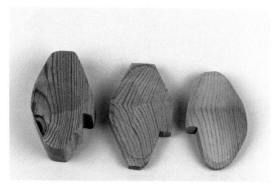

Three stages in shaping a wooden hand.

Grooves were filed into this hand to pick out the fingers.

Painting a slightly shaped hand can be very effective.

A screw-eye and cord wrist joint.

Wooden shapes representing hands

Any wooden shape, like the one illustrated below, can represent a hand. A screw-eye and cord joint can be used for this too. For an alternative to knotting the cord:

1. Insert the cord through the screw-eye and fold the end of the cord back.
2. Glue the two strands of cord together.
3. Tie a strong thread around both pieces of the cord to secure the loop.

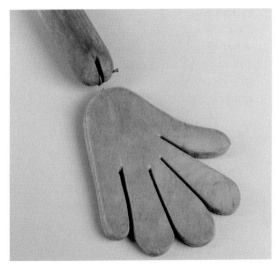

Plywood cut into the shape of a hand.

Hands need not be natural. They can be represented in many ways.

Flat plywood hands

Spare pieces of plywood can be made into flat hands by shaping them with a coping saw. To make the wrist joint for the hand illustrated:

1. Insert a screw-eye of suitable size into the hand at the wrist.
2. Use a saw to cut a slot into the dowelling lower arm.
3. To make the slot wider, cut a second slot next to the first one and remove the waste between the slots with a craft knife.
4. Insert the screw-eye into the slot and secure it in place with a nail through a pre-drilled hole across the forearm.

This joint restricts the hand to movement in only one plane.

A Range of Other Wrist Joints

A thick rope joint

Rope is usually too thick to bend into a loop for a joint, but it can be buried into a hand made from foam rubber. Use a type of foam rubber that adheres with the glue being used.

1. With a sharp knife, cut shallow slots in the palm of the hand.
2. Use scissors to snip away the foam between the slots, leaving a groove.

Grooves cut in foam rubber ready to make the wrist joint.

3. Spread a strong glue along the groove and insert the end of the rope into the groove.
4. When dry, this should provide a secure joint.
5. You can keep the hands in a mitten shape or snip away to create fingers, taking care not to spoil the joint with the rope.

The rope arm is glued securely into the hand.

A cord joint
For materials that do not react well to adhesives, a cord joint in a tubular arm may be used if the hand is sufficiently strong.

1. Pierce a hole through the hand near the wrist.
2. Insert the cord through the hole and knot the ends to form a loop.

3. Tie a strong thread around the loop close to the hand.
4. If you wish, you can glue felt or other fabric around the loop to tidy the wrist joint.
5. Prepare the forearm by making a hole from side to side across the tube at a point where the loop of cord would reach it.

Preparing a cord wrist joint.

The loop of cord is covered with felt to tidy the parts visible to an observer.

6. Insert the loop into the tube and secure it with a nail across the pre-made hole. Secure the head of the nail with glue.

7. As an alternative to the nail, use a piece of coat-hanger wire across the tube and bend the ends over to secure it.

The cord loop is secured in the arm by a nail.

Coat-hanger wire can be used to secure the wrist joint.

A dowel and screw-eye joint
A dowel with a screw-eye in the end can facilitate a wrist joint in various ways.

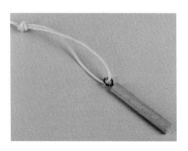

A dowel, screw-eye and cord ready for a wrist joint.

- Make a hole in the hand at the wrist to accommodate the dowel, or glue and sandwich the dowel between two hand sections with grooves made in the same way as for the rope wrist joint described previously. Tie cord to the screw-eye to make the type of joint required.

The dowel is glued and sandwiched between two hand shapes.

- Interlock the screw-eye with another screw-eye attached to the end of the forearm or tie the screw-eyes together with cord.

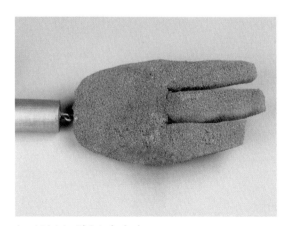

A wrist joint with interlocked screw-eyes.

A wire and cord joint

As an alternative to inserting a dowel into the hand, glue a loop of coat-hanger wire into the hand at the wrist and use the loop for attaching any cord or rope.

A loop of wire glued in the hand is linked to the cord arm.

Hands that do not react well to adhesives

If the hand is created from a type of foam that is not very conducive to gluing:

1. Bend a piece of coat-hanger wire into a 'V' shape, as wide as the hand allows.
2. Insert the wire deep into the hand, leaving just a small loop protruding.
3. Thread the cord through the wire loop to effect the chosen wrist joint.
4. Check that the wire does not slip out of the hand. The 'V' shape should prevent this from happening.

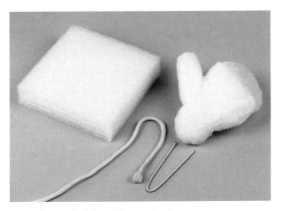

Preparing a wrist joint without adhesive.

The wire in a large 'V' shape does not slip out of the hand.

A strap joint

For this joint, a faux leather or fabric strap fits into slots in the forearm and the hand. It is achieved most conveniently if the forearm is made from a material that is easily cut and responds well to adhesive.

1. Cut a slot in the forearm and glue the strap into it. This is easiest if the strap is wider than needed so that you have something to grip. Trim the waste away when the joint is secure.
2. If required, insert a couple of pins into the forearm and through the strap for extra security.
3. Cut two identical hand shapes from your chosen material.
4. Glue the hand sections to each side of the strap, leaving sufficient space at the wrist to allow movement.

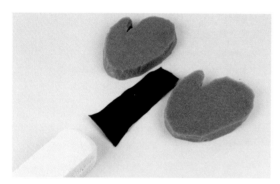

Preparing a wrist joint with faux leather.

The wrist joint assembled. The excess material is trimmed away when the glue has set.

Rod-and-Hand Puppets

These puppets have a human hand, usually gloved. For those with solo operators, the puppeteer provides one hand while holding the puppet's control rod with the other. A second puppeteer may operate one or both hands; this requires careful planning with the main puppeteer.

The puppet may have a costume with sleeves through which the human hand is inserted, or a loose, flowing costume that is gathered around the performer's wrist so that only the gloved hand appears.

A puppet with a gloved human hand. The loosely draped costume hides the performer's arm.

LEGS AND KNEE JOINTS

Many of the methods for making legs and ankle joints are interchangeable with the methods for making arms and wrist joints, as noted previously. Therefore, please refer to the section 'Arms and Elbow Joints' as well as exploring the methods outlined below, which are particularly suitable for legs.

Cord Legs

Simple puppets may have legs made only of cord. Ensure that there is sufficient weight in the feet to achieve a good walking action.

Rope and Foam Rubber Legs

Thick rope is useful as a central core for attaching foam rubber legs, provided it is not too stiff. The legs illustrated cover the rope with insulation tubing that was left over after lagging water pipes. It is particularly easy to use as it has a slot throughout its length which

A puppet inspired by John Roberts' book, *Making Simple Marionettes* (The Crowood Press, 2019).

can be opened and simply popped over the rope. A wedge shape is cut at the knee joint to facilitate bending.

Tubing left after lagging pipes is prepared for a knee joint.

The tubing is glued onto the rope.

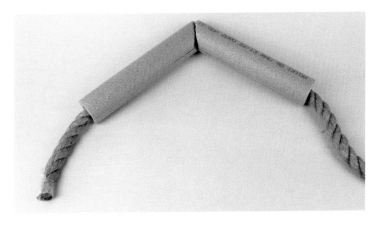

Cardboard Tube Legs

Most of the elbow joints described previously can be used for the knees of cardboard tubes.

The example included here emerged from an experiment by one of the contributors. It has its limitations, but it is an interesting alternative that would suit some circumstances as the idea is to use whatever is available.

Each joint requires four rivet-type paper fasteners and two strips of plastic cut from a thin container. It will help if the plastic is reasonably transparent.

1. Cut a wedge shape from the tubes where the knee will bend.
2. Cut two oval shapes in the plastic. Make them long enough to cover the top and bottom of the knee joint and round off each end.
3. Make holes on each side of the tubing to accommodate the paper fasteners.
4. Place the plastic against the tubing and mark where the holes are.
5. Punch holes in the plastic to correspond to the holes in the tubing. Ensure that the plastic can turn freely on the paper fasteners.

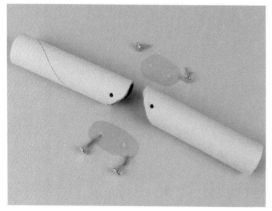

The components of an experiment with a knee joint.

6. Insert the paper fasteners through the hole in the plastic and the cardboard tubes to assemble the joint.
7. Open the fasteners inside the tubing and check that the knee bends smoothly.

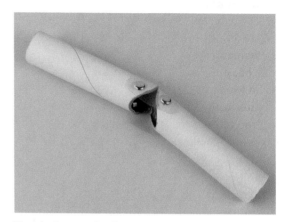

The joint is secured with rivet-type paper fasteners.

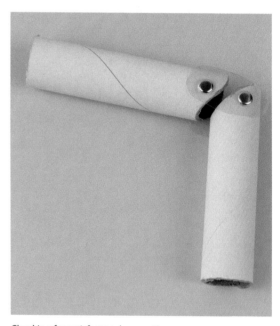

Checking for satisfactory knee action.

A Strap Joint for Foam Rubber Legs

The method of jointing foam rubber arms works well for legs. A wedge is cut away at the back of the knee to allow bending and a strap is glued and inserted into a slot in each section in the same way as the elbows.

Balsa Wood Legs

The same strap joint can be used for all wooden legs, but it is most easily achieved with balsa wood which is easy to cut and can be shaped in minutes with a rasp or glasspaper.

Proceed in the same way as for foam rubber knees and elbows. For extra securing of the joint, after gluing the strap in place, glue and push dressmakers' pins down through the balsa wood and through the strap.

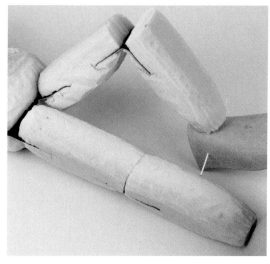

A faux leather joint for foam rubber legs.

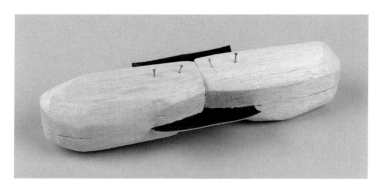

Dressmakers' pins add security to the joint in balsa wood.

The finished joint works well.

MDF Knee Joints

A few small pieces of MDF (or plywood) can be turned into effective knee joints without making entirely wooden legs. It is not of the same standard as a professional wooden leg joint, but it serves its purpose and is easier to make with limited resources.

You will need four strips of MDF of equal width.

1. Draw smooth curves around one end of each of three of the strips and mark the centre-point of the curves.
2. Shape the curves with a coping saw or a rasp and finish smoothing the curves with glasspaper.
3. Drill a hole down through the centre point of the three curves. It will help if you can clamp the three sections together to drill the hole down through them.

4. Cut away a wedge shape from the fourth strip of MDF. It will help the smoothness of the joint if this strip is just a little thicker than the other strips.

5. Arrange the four sections as illustrated with the shorter, cut-away strip between two of the longer strips and the third longer strip facing it.

6. Glue together the two long strips with the shorter, thicker one sandwiched between them.

7. Before the glue has set, insert the third longer strip into the slot created and secure the joint with a nail.

8. The strip should pivot freely in the slot in one direction, but the short central block should prevent it from bending the wrong way. You will have a little while to make some adjustment to the block before the glue sets.

9. Glue the head of the nail to stop it falling out. Cut off the other end when the join has set.

10. Fasten the knee joint into the legs. The illustration shows the joint in use with legs made of cardboard tubes.

11. Cut foam or other padding to fill the space between the knee joint and the tubing.

12. Glue the padding to the leg sections and then glue the entire knee assembly into the tubes.

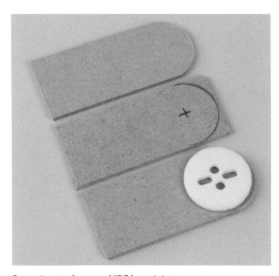

Preparing to shape an MDF knee joint.

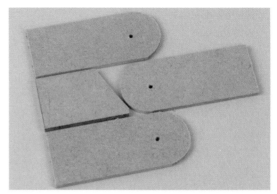

The parts laid out ready for assembling in the order shown. The shortest piece is a little thicker than the other parts.

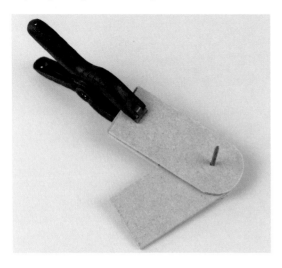

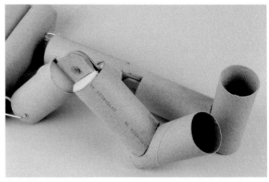

The knee joints are secured inside the leg tubes with suitable packing on both sides.

It helps if the sections are clamped together while the glue is setting.

HIP JOINTS

The joint chosen for hips depends on both the materials used for the body and legs and the amount of control you want over the leg movements.

A simple cord joint
One of the simplest methods to join the legs is to tie them to the body.

1. Pierce holes from side to side near the top of the leg.
2. Insert cord through the holes, leaving equal lengths on each side.
3. Insert each end of the cord through holes made in the body.
4. Pull the cord through until the legs hang and move freely as required.
5. Knot the ends of the cord.

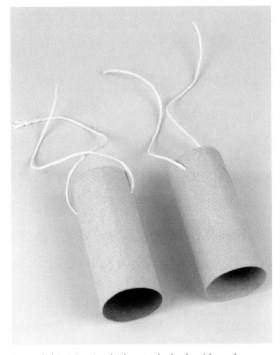

A simple hip joint ties the legs to the body with cord.

Rope hips
Figures that have a continuous piece of rope for the arm and leg have no joint at the hip, but they do need to be held in place.

1. Insert into the bottom of the body packing blocks to the sides and between the legs.
2. Try different arrangements until the legs are positioned as required.
3. Glue the blocks to the body and to the sides of the rope.

A continuous length of rope forms an arm and a leg.

The rope legs are spaced by blocks of any material glued in place.

A wire joint

This hip joint has the legs suspended from a wire that is attached to the body. A spacer between the legs keeps them in position.

1. Pierce holes from side to side near the top of the leg.
2. Pierce a hole midway across what is to be used as a spacer. This could be a block of a solid material or even a ping-pong ball; a piece of plastic tubing will not need piercing.
3. Insert a piece of coat-hanger wire through the holes in the legs with the spacer in between them.

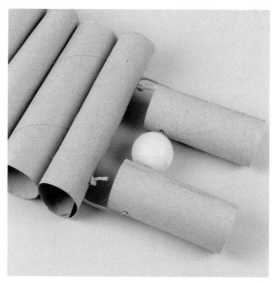

The wire is bent over inside the body tube to secure it.

OR

If the body is a container, place the wire along the sides of the body and bend the ends into another right angle and insert them into the body. Glue and/or tape the wire along the sides of the body.

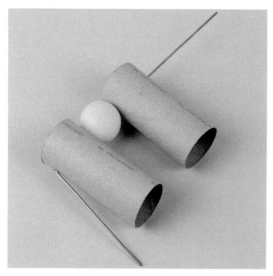

The first stage of making a hip joint with wire.

4. Bend each end of the wire into a right angle, keeping them approximately parallel.
5. Mark the points on the body where you want to insert the wire and make small holes at these points.

The next steps depend on the structure of the body.

6. If the body is hollow tubing, insert the wire into holes in the bottom of the tube and bend the ends to a right angle inside the tube. This part of the process is a little tricky if the wire is too far inside the tube.

The wire through the legs with a tubing spacer. The ends of the wire are bent at right angles and inserted in the sides of the body.

A faux leather or fabric joint

If the body has been built upon a central core of strong material, it is constructed with extra material extending below the hip to join to the legs which are made of a solid material, not hollow.

The central core of this body is extended at the hips to make the joint with the legs.

1. Cut slots from side to side down through the tops of the legs.
2. Insert the material into the slots to check the space between the legs and the body. If it is too close, leg movement will be limited.
3. Trim the material to the length required.
4. If necessary, trim a wedge shape from the tops of the legs at the front to enhance movement.
5. Glue the material into the slots. You can secure the joint further with dressmakers' pins pushed down through the fabric.
6. Trim away the spare material between the legs to enable the legs to move independently of each other.

Slots in the legs are glued to the faux leather, or strong fabric, through the centre of the body.

FEET AND ANKLE JOINTS

When making feet, have due regard for how you plan to make the ankle joint. This will depend on the nature of the legs as well as the feet. Remember that many joints are interchangeable, so you do not have to follow the examples here for a particular material. Consider the different materials involved and the resources available when deciding which ankle joint suits your purposes.

Cardboard tubes
Cardboard tubes provide ready-made feet or shoes. They can remain circular or can be pressed into other shapes. The edges of cardboard tube legs offer very little surface area for glued joints, so they need some assistance.

1. Trim the bottom of the leg to fit snugly over the foot.
2. Glue and insert material padding into the end of the leg. Use foam rubber, wastepaper or any solid material that will adhere with glue.
3. Glue the end of the leg and the padding to the top of the foot.
4. If the legs and feet are to be covered, you may add adhesive tape down the sides of the leg and under the foot to secure the joint.

The bottom of each leg is filled with padding to provide good adhesion to the feet.

The tubular legs are shaped to fit tightly to the feet.

Plastic cartons

Cartons, used on their sides, can be ready-made feet or shoes. Some cartons are comparatively thin and may need padding inside, or covering outside, to strengthen them. If they are to be covered with a material when finished, this may be all the strengthening they require.

1. Ensure that the legs are long enough to fit down to the bottom of the carton.

2. Cut slots into the edge of the carton to create a flap the width of the leg.
3. Bend the flap down and insert the bottom of the leg against it. Increase the slots, if necessary, so that the leg fits fully into the carton.
4. When you are satisfied that it is a good fit, glue the bottom and side of the leg to the carton and the flap. You can strengthen this joint when you add the covering to the foot.

Plastic cups used as the basis for feet.

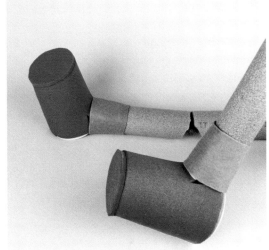

The covering of the feet strengthens the feet and the ankle joint.

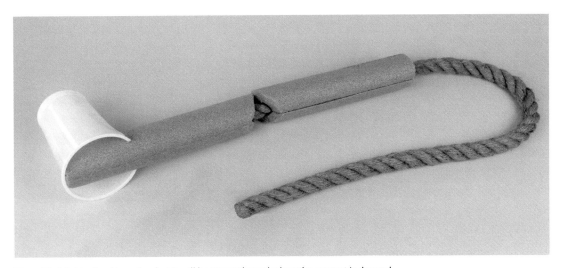

The ankle joint is glued together but it will be strengthened when the puppet is dressed.

Cardboard feet

Cardboard can be shaped, glued and taped into any shape required, but the shaped, recycled cardboard padding often found inside new shoes is a particularly useful basis for instant shoes.

1. Fix a screw-eye into the end of a piece of dowelling.
2. Make a hole up through the bottom of the leg to accommodate the dowel. Glue and insert the dowel into the leg.
3. In the top of the shoe make a hole the same diameter as the dowelling.
4. Insert the dowelling into the shoe through this hole.
5. Pierce small holes in the sides of the shoe and insert a piece of coat-hanger wire crossways through these holes and through the screw-eye in the end of the dowel to secure it in place.

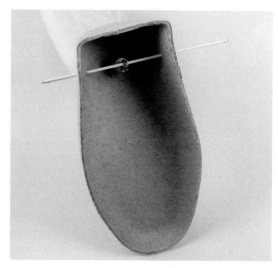

Securing the dowel inside the foot with coat-hanger wire.

6. When you are satisfied that the joint works, bend over the ends of the wire through the foot to secure it and add your chosen covering. This example is covered with faux leather.

The components of an ankle joint with cardboard feet.

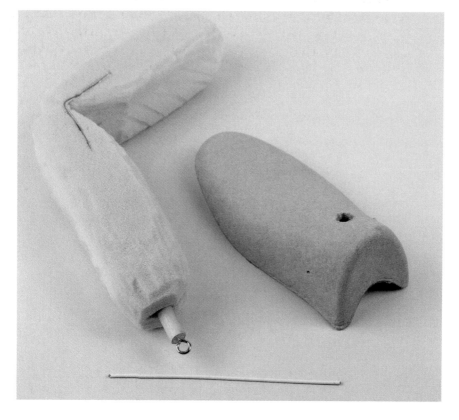

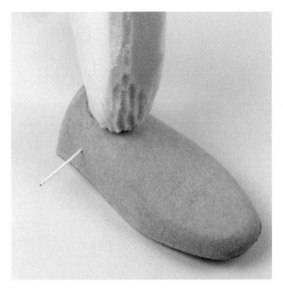

The top of the dowel is glued into the bottom of the leg.

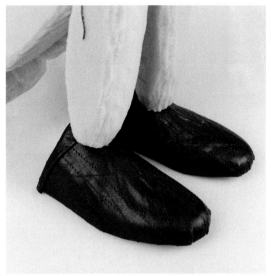

The shoe-shaped cardboard is covered with pieces of faux leather.

Foam rubber feet

Foam rubber can be trimmed into shoes or feet, provided that the major shaping is done with a bread knife (preferably an old one) and scissors are used only for a little extra shaping. There are quick methods for making the ankle joint:

- Cut a hole in the foot exactly the size of the leg and glue the leg in place. It may be helpful to cut the hole a little small at first and gradually enlarge it to avoid making the hole too big from the start. If extra fastening is required, insert a piece of coat-hanger wire across the joint from side to side.

A foot made from packing material. A circle is cut away to take the leg.

The leg should fit tightly in the foot for good adhesion.

- Make corresponding holes in the top of the foot and the bottom of the leg. Glue the bottom of the leg, and glue and insert a dowel rod into both holes to make the joint.

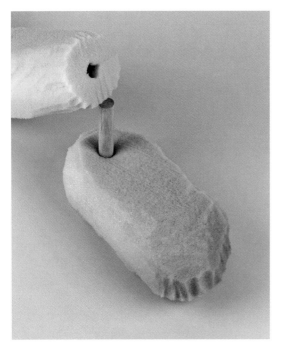

Corresponding holes for a dowel are made in the foot and the leg.

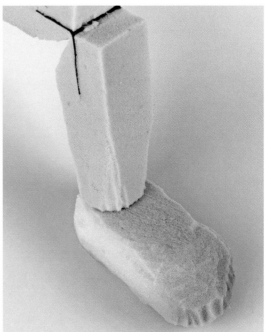

A dowel is glued into the foot and the leg to secure this ankle joint.

Wooden Feet

Off-cuts of wood of any shape may represent feet without being changed, or blocks of wood may be shaped into shoes or feet with tools, as described for wooden hands.

In the example of a bird with cord legs, the end of the cord is glued into holes drilled down through the feet which need sufficient weight to assist control. This bird walks satisfactorily but would not have done so if they had been any lighter.

The larger shaped feet are shown in two stages of construction; a basic outline cut with a saw, and a block shaped with a rasp and smoothed with glasspaper. This process takes a little longer than most.

The shaped foot needs a strong ankle joint such as the one described above for cardboard feet. A dowel with a screw-eye on the end is inserted into a hole in the foot and is secured with a nail or piece of wire inserted across the side of the foot.

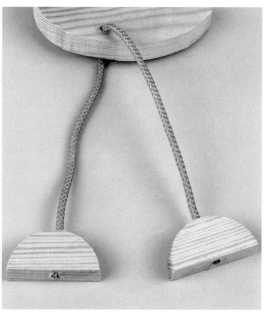

Spare pieces of wood were used for these feet. The cord is glued into holes drilled carefully in the wood.

Two stages in shaping wooden feet.

CHAPTER 4

HAND PUPPETS

This chapter provides examples of how a selection of heads described in Chapter 2 can become different types of hand puppet through quite simple measures. For those who can manage basic sewing, it includes a fabric animal and instructions for creating the 'glove' of a glove puppet.

If a hand puppet is operated with fingers inserted in the neck, it is recommended that two fingers are used, the index and middle fingers. This provides more secure handling of props and the head can be turned by moving alternate fingers backwards and forwards.

IMPROVISED HAND PUPPETS

- A plastic airflow ball takes on human or animal characteristics by inserting it on your index finger, with or without a glove on your hand. Additional features may define the character more, but it is very expressive without them.

- A combination of materials that formed a head were held by a hand with a piece of jersey material draped over it before holding the head. The angle of the puppeteer's fingers, hand and arm, and the extent to which the fabric covers or surrounds part of the head, enables the puppet to adopt a range of different characteristics. Because the fabric is only draped and not cut in any way, it is possible to use it again and again for other puppets at other times.

A simple ball on a gloved hand demonstrates the involvement of the onlooker in interpreting this as a character with personality and feelings.

A hand draped in fabric holds this improvised head to create a character. Changing the angle at which it is held changes the character, its age, and requires a different character voice.

OPPOSITE: Cardboard cones with a tape hinge create a moving mouth for a simple finger puppet.

FINGER PUPPETS

- A fabric finger puppet also provides the choice of being used with or without a gloved hand. As it is made from felt, there will be a little flexibility in the puppet, which you might find easier to achieve without a glove.

Manipulation of the finger puppet might be easier and more flexible without a gloved hand. The performer can decide.

- The conical finger puppet seems to be more effective with a gloved hand. The shape suggests an animal, but it can work as well as a human, particularly if the operating hand is more upright.
- A finger puppet with a moving mouth is made from two of the same cones hinged together with strong adhesive tape and decorated. It is operated with your index finger on top and your thumb below.

Alternatively, you can make the cones wider and flatter to accommodate two fingers in the top half if this is more comfortable.

Joining two cardboard cones with a tape hinge creates a moving mouth.

This finger puppet is more convincing with a gloved hand, which becomes the puppet's body.

The mouth made with hinged cones is operated by the index finger and thumb in the top and bottom jaws respectively.

OTHER HAND PUPPETS

- A sock puppet is ready to perform as soon as you insert your hand, though you might need to ensure it is tucked in well to form the mouth. Gluing a lining into the mouth usually ensures it is ready to perform without any adjustment needed.
- A paper plate sleeve puppet is another puppet that is ready to perform as soon as you slip your hand into the mouth. If you make the 'sleeve' part looser/wider, you can attach padding to your arm inside the sleeve to give the body more shape.

Manipulate a sock puppet with your wrist bent to relate to the audience. Avoid performing as if it is staring at the sky.

- A cheesebox head needs only a body to be ready to perform. Drape a piece of fabric over your index and middle fingers and insert them into the neck.

  The draped fabric creates a basic body without arms or hands, but mitten-type hands can be created very easily as demonstrated with the following puppet, or the head can be attached to a traditional glove which is described at the end of this chapter.

  In the following chapter, the same head becomes both a rod puppet and a rod-and-hand puppet.

- An eggbox hand puppet also needs only fabric draped over the hand that is inserted into the box. Provided the fabric is not too thick or stiff, elastic bands over fabric-covered fingers create hands for the puppet.

A simple drape serves as the puppet's body. With this method a change of costume is possible and the fabric can be used repeatedly.

This puppet has quite a slim body unless padding is attached to the arm to create a body shape.

Elastic bands are used over the performer's finger(s) and thumb to establish hands quickly for the eggbox hand puppet.

Alternatively, the head may be combined with a traditional glove puppet body or used for a hand-and-rod puppet, both of which are detailed below.

- The plastic bottle animal was operated with the performer's arm covered by the thick sleeve of a dark sweater. If the puppet is doing something interesting, the observer tends to focus on this and accepts the method of manipulation as if it were invisible.

- A fur fabric animal is a simple tube shape that is tapered towards the nose and stitched together with the fur inside out.

The eyes and nose were commercially produced for dolls. Their points are pushed through the material and secured with studs that snap on. Then the figure is turned back the right way and is ready to perform.

This furry animal immediately gets a friendly response from its audience.

The hand puppet made from a bottle needs only the insertion of a hand with a covered sleeve to be ready to perform.

The tapered faux fur is reversed and stitched together down the underside.

The nose and eyes are secured in place before the puppet is reversed with the seam inside.

The operating hand gives shape to this flat puppet.

A hand-and-rod puppet

This makes use of the eggbox head with a child's sweater as the core that connects all the parts. Create the parts from any materials that are available; you do not need these specific items.

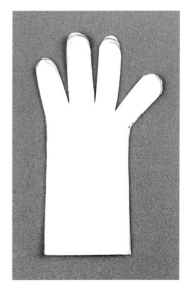

A hand template used to draw on sheet foam; puppets often have fewer fingers than humans.

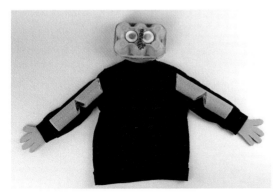

The eggbox head is given a child's sweater, arms and hands to convert it into a hand-and-rod puppet.

Materials: sweater, sheet foam rubber, foam rubber pipe lagging, thin dowel rods, paper clips, buttons, strong thread.

1. Make a paper template for the hands. Remember that puppets often have three fingers rather than four, so you need not follow human characteristics.
2. Use the template to draw the hands on the chosen material and cut them out.
3. Secure the hands in the sleeves of the sweater. You can pin or stitch them in place temporarily or glue them in permanently.
4. To make the dowelling control rods for the hands, open small paper clips to form a 'U' shape to fit along the sides of the dowels and trim away any excess wire. Glue and tape the paper clips to the rods, leaving a small loop protruding.

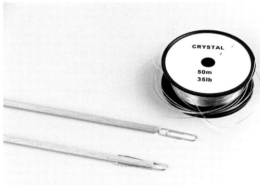

Thin rods, topped with pieces of paper clips, are prepared for use as hand control rods.

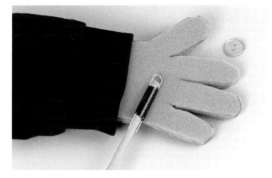

Attach the rod to a suitable point on the hand to maximise control.

5. Attach the wire loops to the palms of the hands with strong thread through the hands and secured to buttons on the back of the hands. Secure the knots with glue.

6. Insert one hand through the sweater and into the egg box while operating the hands with the control rods.

The hand rods are attached, using buttons to prevent the thread pulling through the sheet foam hands.

The head may be attached permanently to the rest of the puppet or may be fitted into the hand temporarily so that it can be used in other ways.

A 'GLOVE' FOR A GLOVE PUPPET

A tin can head here demonstrates the recommended manipulation method for glove puppets, with and without the glove puppet body which has a neutral appearance ready for any costume to be added.

A demonstration of the recommended glove puppet manipulation technique for which the 'glove' is required.

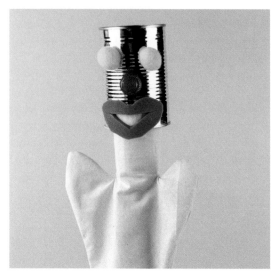

The 'glove' body designed for a good fit for the neck and on whichever hand it is operated.

Materials that might be used for the costume may not be the best, or the easiest to use, for making the glove, which is why puppeteers usually make the glove from a fabric that is hard wearing without being stiff. Curtain lining or jersey material are particularly good examples; for the puppet illustrated, calico was used.

It is advisable to make a paper template for the glove. For this, you need to decide whether to make a glove that will fit a particular hand or to fit both hands. It will be a better fit if made for one hand but will give more scope for performance if the puppet can be used comfortably on either hand.

The glove should reach down almost to your elbow if you do not want your arm or wrist to appear while performing.

A loop of wire stitched into the hem provides a means to hang the puppet up and holds the hem open for easy insertion of your hand when performing.

Making the glove
Materials: fabric, sheet of paper, sewing cottons/threads, coat-hanger wire.

1. Place your hand on a sheet of paper with your hand in the operating position and draw around the outline but not too close to the hand. Ensure that the neck will be wide enough to fit over the puppet's neck and allow a margin of about 2cm around the hand and 3cm on each side of the arm so that the glove will be wide enough for you to insert and remove your hand easily.
2. If the glove needs to fit both hands, turn your hand over and draw the outline again, then make a smooth curve around both outlines.
3. Cut out the pattern and place it on a double piece of material, inside out. Draw around the outline.
4. It is recommended that beginners run a tacking stitch around this outline and try the glove for size before cutting it out, so that it can be unpicked and adjusted if necessary.

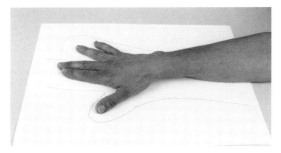

Draw an outline for the glove not too close to the hand and arm on which it will be used.

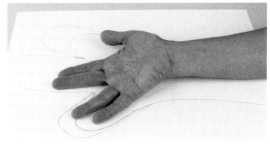

Repeat the process with the hand reversed if the puppet is to be used on each hand.

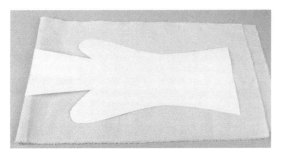

The paper pattern is placed on a double sheet of fabric which should reach to the performer's elbow.

The double fabric is tacked together for checking the fit before the glove is stitched permanently.

5. Stitch along both sides of the glove by hand or machine, leaving the top and bottom open.

6. Cut out the glove within about 5mm of the stitching and snip right into the corners between the neck and arms, as close as possible to the stitching without cutting it. This reduces any puckering when the glove is reversed.

7. Bend a long piece of coat-hanger wire into a loop and form a circle with the remainder of the wire to fit inside the bottom of the glove while it is still inside out, as illustrated. Turn the hem up around the wire and pin it in place ready for securing.

8. Glue and/or stitch the hem around the wire, then reverse the glove so that the seams are inside.

9. Glue or tie the glove to the puppet's neck or hold it in place with a tight elastic band so that you can use it for different puppets.

A loop of wire is fixed into the hem to hold the glove open and provide a hook for hanging it.

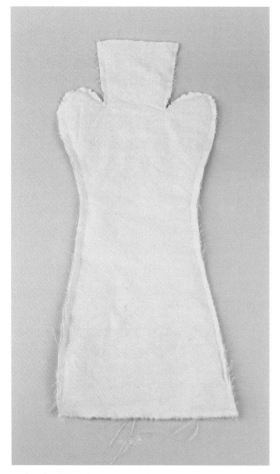

Each side of the glove is stitched together, leaving the top and bottom open. Excess fabric is trimmed away.

The glove is reversed and the hem is sealed.

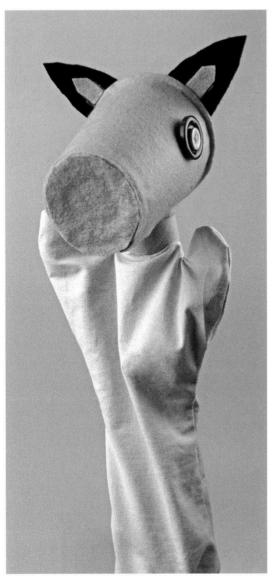

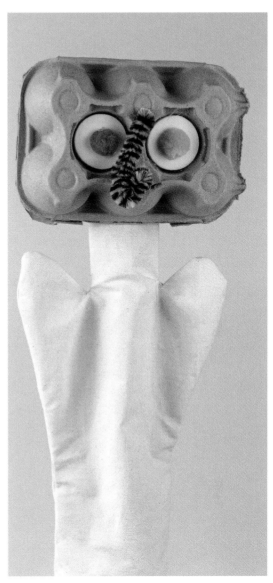

The glove is attached to one of the animal heads ready for a costume to be added.

The eggbox head has now been returned to use as a glove puppet.

CHAPTER 5

ROD PUPPETS

Many of the heads described in Chapter 2 are suitable for rod puppets. The difference between a head for a hand puppet, a rod puppet, or a marionette is often related to whether the neck needs to accommodate two fingers, a rod, or an attachment to the body.

Rod puppets can be made with a full body and limbs, rather like a marionette, so you will find examples in Chapter 6 if this is required. However, the popular convention that rod puppets appear to waist or hip level is particularly helpful for quickly made puppets as it is half the work.

The puppets described here use a combination of materials and methods for the bodies and limbs that are outlined in Chapter 3. You may not have identical materials and you do not need to use the same combinations. Understand the structure of each rod puppet described here and look through Chapter 3 to see which of the methods will suit the materials that you have for what you want to achieve.

Before making any rod puppet, determine the length of the central rod. As noted previously, a puppet with a long rod cannot bend at the waist; to effect waist movements, use a shorter rod and hold it with the hand up inside the costume. This makes a wider range of movements possible.

SIMPLE ROD PUPPETS

A Wooden Spoon Rod Puppet

Wooden spoon puppets need not have any costume; they are ready to use as they are. A rod puppet without a body is like a marot (or marotte), the jester's stick from the Middle Ages.

Alternatively, a simple costume may be added, draped around the rod and secured at the neck by an elastic band. In Chapter 2 this same puppet was shown with the puppeteer's thumb and index finger stretched out inside the costume to suggest a body or shoulders.

A draped costume for a simple rod puppet without a body or limbs.

OPPOSITE: A common type of rod puppet without legs. It is visible at waist- or hip-height when performed behind a screen but could be used in the open with the performer visible.

95

A Free-Standing Carton Puppet

A finger puppet or any other head, such as the tin can, can be popped onto a fabric-covered rod to make it into a rod puppet but they can also be used as free-standing characters for performing on any surface.

An easy way to do this is to stand the supporting rod in a bottle or fit the puppet's neck over the neck of a bottle. Ensure the bottle is steady or add a little ballast, such as sand. The puppets are held and moved from the bottom of the bottle and may be stood in a display when not in use.

A finger puppet can double as a rod puppet and the rod can stand in a bottle as a free-standing figure.

A hand puppet head is supported on a bottle to become free standing.

The fabric is gathered around the neck with a draw-thread, so it can be removed easily and re-used.

A Simple Paper Plate Rod Puppet

Materials: paper plate, an old stick or rod, strips of card, fabric and trimmings.

Attach a dowel rod to the back of the decorated plate with strips of card glued on. Secure the card with clothes pegs while the glue is drying. Adhesive tape is an alternative to glued card, but it may not adhere for as long.

The character may be used with or without a simple costume or made into a more substantial rod puppet as described below.

The puppet can be used to perform with or without a body or costume.

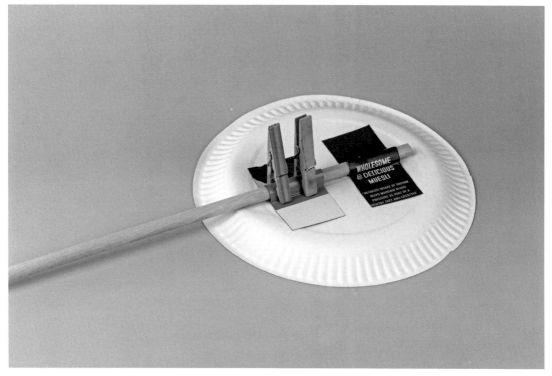

Securing a rod to a paper plate head with strips of card glued in place.

STANDARD ROD PUPPETS

A paper plate rod puppet

Attach the head to the central rod as described above and insert a piece of tubing for the neck onto the rod. Add a shoulder block, arms and hands. This puppet has padded carton shoulders supported on the rod by a circular block of foam rubber.

The arms are plastic tubes separated by wooden balls and threaded onto one piece of cord that runs from wrist to wrist. The hands are shaped plastic foam with a loop of wire inserted to effect the wrist joint.

Make the hand controls as follows:
1. Fix a screw-eye in the top of a dowel rod for each hand.
2. Tie a small button to a piece of strong thread and, with a needle, insert the thread from the back of the hand through to the palm.
3. Tie the thread to the screw-eye in the dowel.

Add any costume, as required.

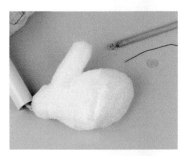

A dowel rod, thread and button prepared for attaching the hand control.

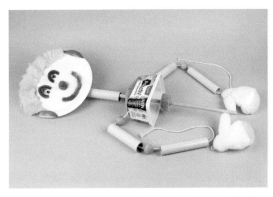

Loosely attached components for adding a body and limbs.

Strong thread attached to a screw-eye in the dowel is fed through to the back of the hand.

Assembly is complete with the arms sufficiently loose to allow free movement.

Thread through the button secures the attachment of the hand control.

A ball and carton rod puppet

Materials: plastic ball, cord, carton, two dowel rods of different lengths, two wooden hemispheres, two screw-eyes, two slices of thick tubing, four short plastic tubes, two garden stakes, two small staples.

1. Fix the central rod into the ball head and insert the short dowel for the nose.
2. Insert the rod into the neck tubing.
3. Thread the arm cord through holes made in the carton shoulder block.
4. Secure the carton on the central rod with a supporting collar.

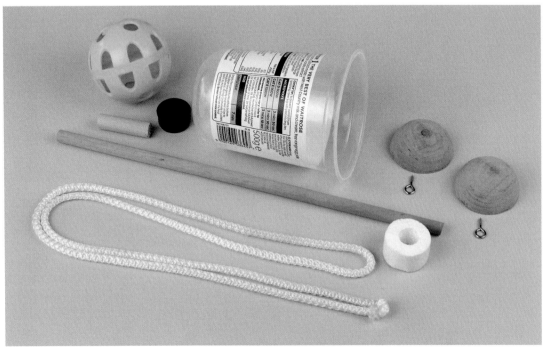

Materials organised ready to construct a ball and carton rod puppet.

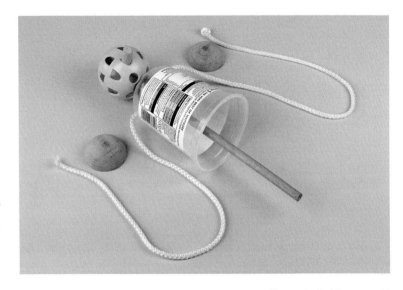

The body is secured on the rod and a single cord for the arms is inserted through holes made at the shoulders.

5. Add the tubes for the arms on the cord, screw the screw-eyes into the wooden hemispheres for the hands and loop the cord through the screw-eyes to make the wrist joints.

   The hand controls are made from garden stakes:

6. Open out a paper clip and cut away the excess, leaving a 'U' shape.

7. Fit the clip to the top of the garden stake and glue and tape it in place.

8. Insert a staple through the loop at the top of the control and tap the staple into the centre of each hand.

9. Drape fabric over the shoulder block and arms for the costume.

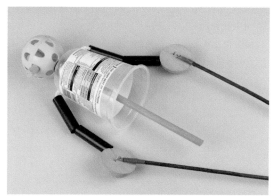

The hand controls are attached using small staples tapped into the palms of the hands.

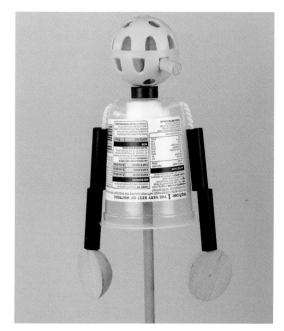

Four plastic tubes become the arms which are secured when the hands are attached.

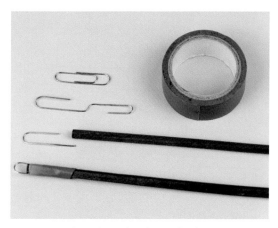

Preparing garden stakes as hand control rods, using paper clips and adhesive tape.

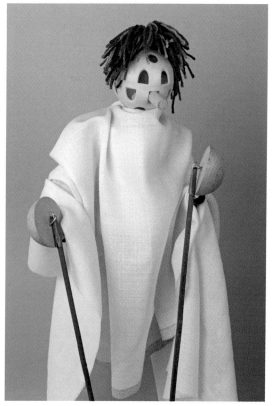

The completed rod puppet with a draped costume.

A rod puppet with a bottle body

Materials: polystyrene ball, long, thin dowel rod, tights, foam rubber tubing, plastic bottle.

1. Make the puppet from a fabric-covered polystyrene head on a long rod with slices of foam rubber tubing for the neck. The fabric covering is a leg cut from a pair of thick tights.

2. Insert the rod through the entire length of the plastic bottle and pull the leg of the tights over the bottle to accentuate its shape.

3. Complete the character with any type of arms, hands and control rods, together with hair and features.

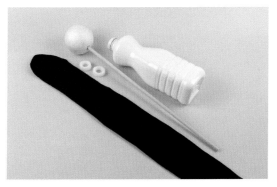

Materials prepared for a puppet with a bottle body.

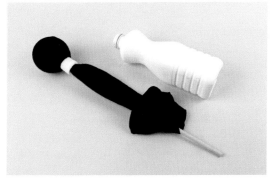

A ball head, with a rod inserted, is covered with a leg from a pair of tights and secured in place.

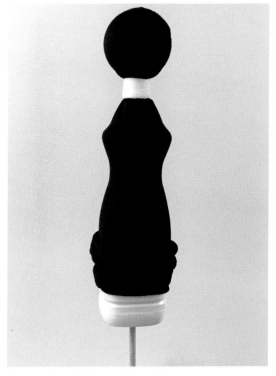

The rod is inserted through the bottle.

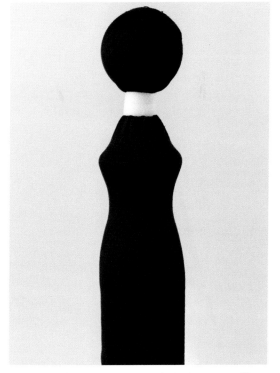

The stretchy fabric accentuates the body shape created by the bottle which is yet to have features and limbs added.

A large rod puppet

1. Following examples in previous chapters, create the head from a large, inverted carton together with a shoulder block, bottle arms and cardboard hands. Attach it to a broom handle with a foam rubber supporting collar glued under the shoulder block.

2. Add the costume before attaching the hand controls which are made from coat-hanger wire and two short dowel rods.

3. Make the coat-hanger wire as straight as possible and bend one end into a small loop. Seal the knot with glue.

4. Drill small holes down into each dowel rod for the handles and glue the ends of the control wires into the dowels. They should be a tight fit.

5. Attach the loops on the control wire to the hands with buttons and threads, as described for a paper plate rod puppet, above.

The large carton head, with a cardboard tube for the neck, is fixed on an old broom handle.

Shoulders and limbs are held in place by a supporting collar.

Coat-hanger wire with a looped end is the hand control.

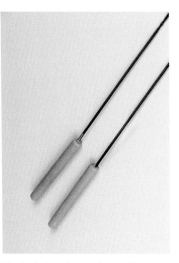

Manipulating the hand controls is helped if the ends are glued into dowel rod handles.

The puppet is dressed in a child's old shirt and is ready to perform.

A simple turning head

Materials: plastic carton, dowel rod, foam rubber tubing, shoulder block, plastic discs from lids.

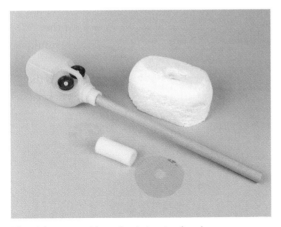

Materials prepared for a simple turning head.

1. Add features to an inverted bottle and secure the bottle on the central rod as described for Rod Puppet Neck Joints.
2. Select a suitable shoulder block and make a hole down through the centre for the main control rod; the example uses a block of polystyrene.
3. Cut two discs from plastic lids and cut central holes for the control rod.
4. Insert the rod through the shoulder block with the plastic discs above and below it to help smooth turning.

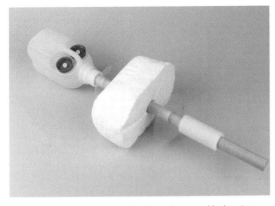

The shoulder block has plastic discs above and below it to assist smooth turning of the head.

5. Slip a supporting collar (here it is foam rubber tubing) onto the rod and glue it in place below the shoulder block and disc. It should be tight enough to keep the shoulder block level, but not too tight or it will hinder turning.
6. Proceed to add limbs, costume and hand controls as for any rod puppet.

Turning the control rod turns the head. Before adding the arms, the costume and hand controls, you may find that the shoulder block turns with the head but, when the puppet is finished, the weight of the additions will hold the shoulders in place and the hand controls help with this, allowing the head to turn independently.

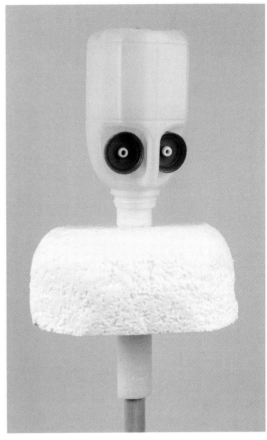

With the supporting collar secured, the head is free to turn independently of the body.

A two-handed turning head

This method of operation is suited to manipulation by two people; one to support the puppet and control the head while the other controls the hands.

Materials: as for the previous turning head, plus a cardboard tube, adhesive tape.

1. Fix a head on the end of a rod, as before.
2. Glue and tape a shoulder block to a long cardboard tube with the top of the tube projecting above the shoulders for the neck.

The internal diameter of the tube should be sufficient to accommodate the head rod and the tube needs to be shorter than the head rod by at least the width of a hand.

3. Place on the head rod a plastic disc cut from a lid and insert the rod into the cardboard tube.
4. Hold the tube with one hand and turn the head rod with the other. You can also raise and lower the head a little for effect.
5. Add limbs, costume and hand controls as required.

The head rod turns freely inside a cardboard tube to which the shoulder block is secured.

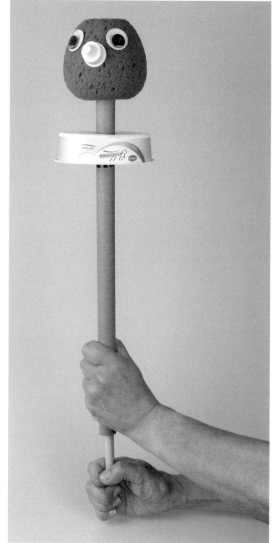

Two hands are needed to support the puppet and control the head, but this will suit some applications. This arrangement might involve two-person coordination to operate the puppet.

A one-handed turning head
This method of head control frees one hand to
operate the hand rods.

Materials: as for the previous turning head, plus
a short piece of coat-hanger wire, a cork or a
small wooden ball.

1. Fix a head on the end of a rod, as before.
2. Insert the head rod into a cardboard or
   plastic tube and mark a convenient position
   for holding it.
3. Cut a slot in the tube at this point.
4. Insert the rod into the tube with the slot aligned
   directly with the back of the head. Allow a little
   space between the top of the tube and the head.
   Mark on the rod the position of the slot.
5. Make a small hole in the rod at the centre
   point of where the slot is drawn.
6. Insert the head rod back into the tube. You
   can add a shoulder block at this point, as
   before; it has been omitted here for clarity.

The head is attached to a piece of broom handle that fits the
internal width of a strong cardboard tube.

The component
parts are
prepared with
a slot cut in the
tube where
the operator
would hold it.
A small hole
is made in the
rod where the
slot would be.

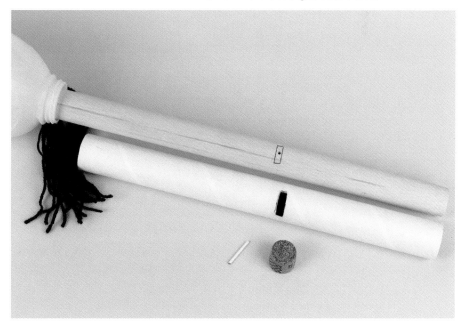

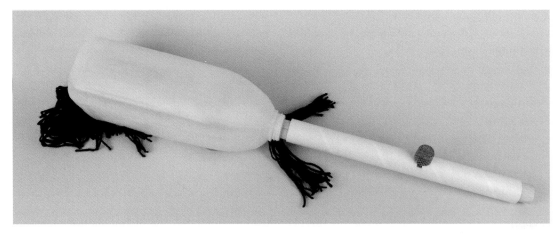

A short piece of wire is glued into the slot and the cork to make a thumb rest.

7. Glue a short piece of coat-hanger wire into the small hole in the rod and glue the other end into a piece of cork or a small, pre-drilled wooden ball, to act as a thumb rest.
8. Hold the tube with one hand with a thumb on the cork to turn the head from side to side.
9. Complete the rod puppet by any of your chosen methods.

The control is held with a thumb on the cork to turn the head from side to side.

A nodding head

Materials: carton head, coat-hanger wire, cardboard tubing or a dowel rod, tubing spacers, thread, small ring to fit a thumb.

1. Drill a small hole across the top of the tubing (or a rod).
2. Make a hole in each side of the carton that is to be the head. Make the holes a little towards the back, rather than in the centre, so that the head falls forwards when attached to the tubing.
3. Push a piece of coat-hanger wire through one side of the head, through the top of the tube with small tubing spacers on each side of it, and out the other side of the head, so that the carton pivots on the tube.
4. Bend over the ends of the wire to secure the joint. This will be hidden by any subsequent head covering or by the ears.
5. Tie strong thread to a small hole in the back of the head carton.

Materials prepared for making a nodding head.

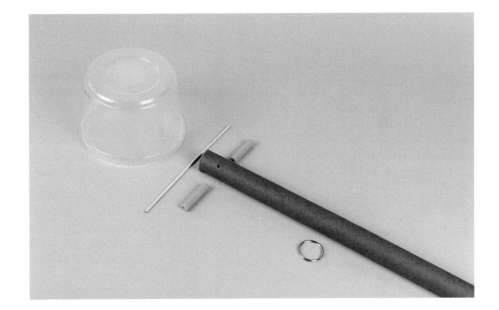

The carton is pivoted on top of the rod with a control cord attached to the back of the head.

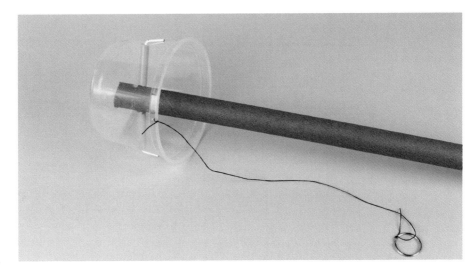

6. Tie the other end of the thread to any sort of ring that will fit comfortably on your thumb.
7. Arrange the length of the thread so that it is taut when the head is looking down.
8. Hold the cardboard tube with your thumb in the ring on the end of the thread. Use your thumb to raise the head and hold it in any position. The weight of the head will bring it forwards when the tension on the thread is relaxed.
9. If you need to limit the degree to which the head moves, glue or tape a little packing inside the front and/or back of the carton.

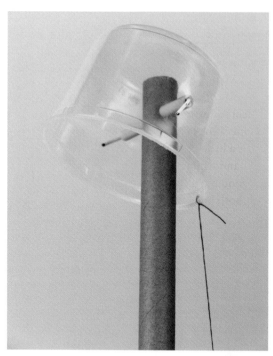

The control string raises the head and holds it in any position.

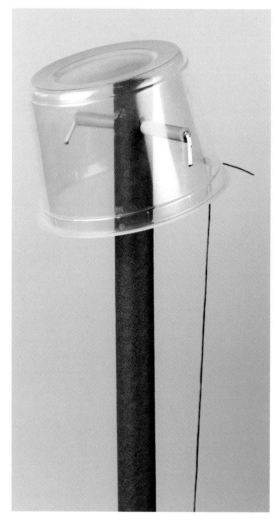

The pivot is arranged so that the weight of the head pulls it forwards.

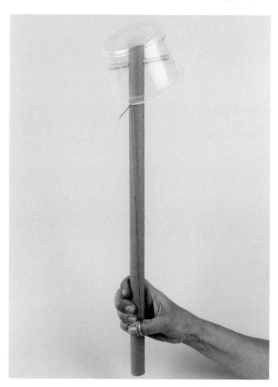

The head is operated with either a finger or thumb of the hand holding the rod.

ROD PUPPET MANIPULATION

Hold the central control rod in either hand and use this to effect movements of the head and the body. Many people prefer to manage the hand controls with their dominant hand and hold the central rod with the other.

Operating two hand controls with one hand needs a little practice. Although you can operate one hand while the other hangs loose, this is not good technique, so it is worth persevering with both hand controls together. First, hold the hand controls together in a comfortable position and you may find that the hands are nicely spread. Then close your fingers around the rods to bring the hands together.

Next, hold the rods together with your thumb resting on the space between them, then spread the rods apart in a slight V-shape with your thumb, and finally spread them wide with your thumb and index finger hooked between them. This method is shown here using dowel rods and hand wires set in dowelling handles.

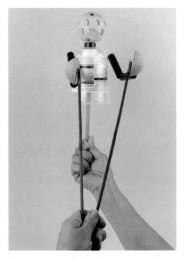

The central rod is held in one hand while the other hand operates the puppet's hands.

Holding the hand controls together brings the hands close.

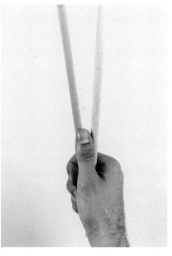

Use a thumb to control the spread of the controls.

Use thumb and index finger to spread the rods apart.

Practise the same manipulation with wires in dowel handles.

Some people prefer one type of control over another.

A TABLE-TOP PUPPET

The reference to 'table-top' carries the notion of modest-sized figures, which is the case for many such puppets. They may be operated by one, two or even three performers and they offer economy of scale for weight, staging, props, transport and the space needed for the performance. They also provide comfortable viewing for a larger audience than most people expect.

However, they do not have to be small. They may be any size that will fit on the chosen playing surface and that the performers can manage, so the combined weight of the puppet, and therefore the materials used, should be considered. Be warned that larger puppets require a lot more space for performing and storage: if you double the size of a puppet and correspondingly double the size of the three-dimensional props, each prop now takes eight times more space (compare 10cm cubed with 20cm cubed).

The two puppets included here were made with lightweight materials throughout but, in each case, there was sufficient weight to facilitate good manipulation. The techniques for making each of the figures are described fully in Chapter 2, Materials, Tools, Heads and Costumes and in Chapter 3, Bodies, Limbs and Joints.

One figure has a head control rod and hand control wires set in dowelling handles. These wires are attached to the hands through the wrists to enable control from behind. The legs are controlled by a puppeteer moving the feet by hand. It could have a separate control to the heels if required.

The puppet that is sculpted entirely from foam rubber has a short main control rod from the head to the middle of the torso. The puppeteer inserts a hand into the torso to control the head and the major body movements. The limbs are controlled by the puppeteers directly holding and moving the limbs with gloved hands. This is a convention that audiences quickly accept, with the performers acting 'on behalf of' the puppet.

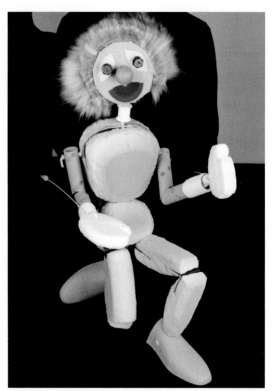

A table-top puppet assembled prior to costuming. Controls would normally be black but have been left visible for the illustrations.

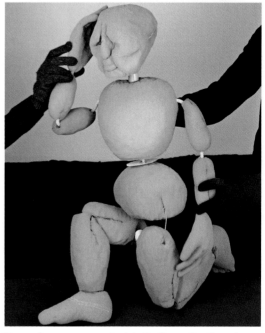

The performers can manipulate the figure directly and handle objects 'on behalf of' the puppet.

A ROD-AND-HAND PUPPET

This type of puppet replaces the puppet's hand(s) with human hand(s). It is usual to wear gloves for the hands as it is more in keeping with the nature of a puppet.

Two operators working together enable the puppet to have two hands. This requires careful co-ordination: either one person works the main control while another works both hands, or one person handles the main control and one hand while the other person provides the second hand, which may be easier to co-ordinate.

The example here is based on the cheesebox head that was made initially as a hand puppet. It demonstrates that the same head can be adapted successfully for different types of puppet.

Making a rod and hand puppet

Materials: as for previous rod puppets plus a glove to fit the performer.

1. Insert a short rod into the puppet's neck and down through a shoulder block, which is made here from a sponge.
2. Drape fabric around the shoulder block and the character becomes a rod puppet. Ensure that there is sufficient fabric for the next stages.
3. Hold the rod with one hand and use your other hand, gloved, for the puppet's hand.
4. Decide where on the robe the hand looks best and note this position with dressmakers' pins.
5. If the fabric may be used again for other purposes, secure it with small safety pins that are carefully positioned or use a few small stitches that can be unpicked. Otherwise, make a slit to insert the hand and glue or stitch the edges to prevent fraying.

The cheesebox hand puppet acquires a rod and a shoulder block.

A substantial piece of fabric is draped around the shoulder block.

A gloved human hand becomes the puppet's hand. Two-person operation is required if the character needs two hands.

ANIMAL ROD PUPPETS

Animals that have a similar structure to humans are made in the same way as other rod puppets. Those that walk on four legs require a different approach.

A rod puppet cat or dog

Materials: plastic cartons, cardboard tube, two dowel rods, drawing pins, plastic and foam tubing, fabric and trimmings.

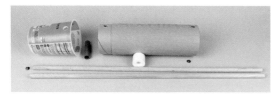

Materials used for a rod puppet animal.

1. Make two holes near the front rim of the body tube, one at the top and one at the bottom, immediately below it. It should be just large enough for the dowel rod to pass through.
2. Make another hole through the bottom of the cardboard tube, near the back.

3. Glue the top of one of the dowel rods and insert it through the hole at the back of the tube. Press it fully against the top of the tube and insert a drawing pin down through the tube to hold the rod in place. If necessary, glue and push a little foam rubber into the bottom of the tube around the rod to help secure it.
4. Insert the other dowel rod, which should be longer, through the two holes at the front of the tube and out through the top for attaching the head and neck.
5. Insert the neck tube onto the dowel and secure the carton head on the top of the rod, as described for other carton rod puppets.
6. Glue a supporting collar on the head rod underneath, and close to, the body but allowing it to turn freely.
7. Remember that rod puppets often have no legs and appear only at the waist so you can simply cover the body with fabric or fur fabric which hangs a little below the body but, if you wish, you can add legs and feet as described for other puppets, such as marionettes.
8. Finish the puppet with features and trimmings.

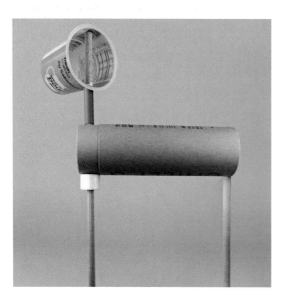

To permit turning, one rod is fixed inside the head and to the supporting collar. The other rod supports the tail.

Fringed fabric covers the body and replaces the need for legs. Face, features, hair and a tail complete the creation of a cat.

A rod puppet bird

Rod puppet birds are often comparatively simple figures that rely upon natural movement effected through the central rod, rather than having additional controls to move the wings.

Materials: polystyrene egg, cardboard tube, long dowel rod, short dowel rod, screw-eye, sheet foam rubber, coat-hanger wire, rivet-type paper fasteners, fabric, trimmings.

1. Use a cardboard tube for the body of the bird. Make small holes horizontally across the tube near one end and near the mid-point.
2. Drill a hole across the top of a long dowel rod and insert this at an angle into a hole made in the underside of the tube, aligning it with the horizontal holes at the mid-point.
3. Insert the rod into this hole and secure it with a piece of coat-hanger wire inserted through the tube and bend over the ends of the wire.
4. Insert a screw-eye into the end of the short dowel and glue the full length of the dowel into a hole made in the polystyrene egg. The angle of this hole will determine the angle of the head, so consider different angles before making the hole.

5. Insert the protruding screw-eye into the end of the body tube, secure it with a piece of coat-hanger wire through the small holes, and bend over the ends, as before.
6. Trim the sheet of foam rubber into the shape of the wings and glue it to the top of the body tube.
7. For extra security, make small holes down through the centre of the wings and the body tube, insert rivet-type paper fasteners and open them inside the tubing.
8. Glue fabric on top of the wings and add trimmings and facial features to the head.

Sheet foam rubber is the basis of the wings, which are glued onto the body. Paper fasteners provide extra security.

The addition of fabric and trimmings transforms the bird completely.

The control rod and the head (which contains a short dowel with a screw-eye in the end) are both secured to the body tube by short pieces of wire.

A flexible rod puppet animal

This puppet can be constructed from a variety of materials and the head could be one of many of those described in Chapter 2. This example uses wooden balls of different sizes and wooden discs with the minimum of additions, which emphasises that a simple head with little embellishment can take on a convincing character.

A similar body could be made with foam rubber or cardboard discs separated by foam rubber spacers, or even scrunched-up net fabric. Cotton reels work well too, like the snake marionette in Chapter 6.

Materials: discs of cardboard, foam rubber, wood or cotton reels, cord, two long dowel rods, two screw-eyes, wooden ball/beads or foam rubber spacers, trimmings.

1. Thread the head, the screw-eyes and the circular discs onto a central cord with small wooden balls or beads between each disc to give the required flexibility. The screw-eye eyes should be on the cord just before the head and towards the end of the tail.

2. Make a small guide hole in the top of each dowel rod and fix the screw-eyes through these holes to secure the control rods.

3. Knot the ends of the cord at the head and tail, glue the knots and trim away any excess cord. You can cover the knots or make them a feature when you add any trimmings.

4. You can cover the body with any material of your choice, but it is common practice to leave it uncovered or simply painted.

Pre-drilled wooden discs and balls make up most of this flexible rod puppet.

A ROD-MARIONETTE

Rod puppets are sometimes operated from above, like marionettes. The flexible rod puppet detailed above can be a rod-marionette too. It is constructed in the same way but operated with the control rods pointing down rather than upwards. It could be performed with other similar figures or alongside marionettes.

Some rod-marionettes are made more like the marionettes described in Chapter 6. They often have a central rod down to the head and body and a mixture of strings and/or rods to the hands. Any combination is possible so you could experiment and create your own mix.

The same puppet can be used as a rod-marionette operated from above.

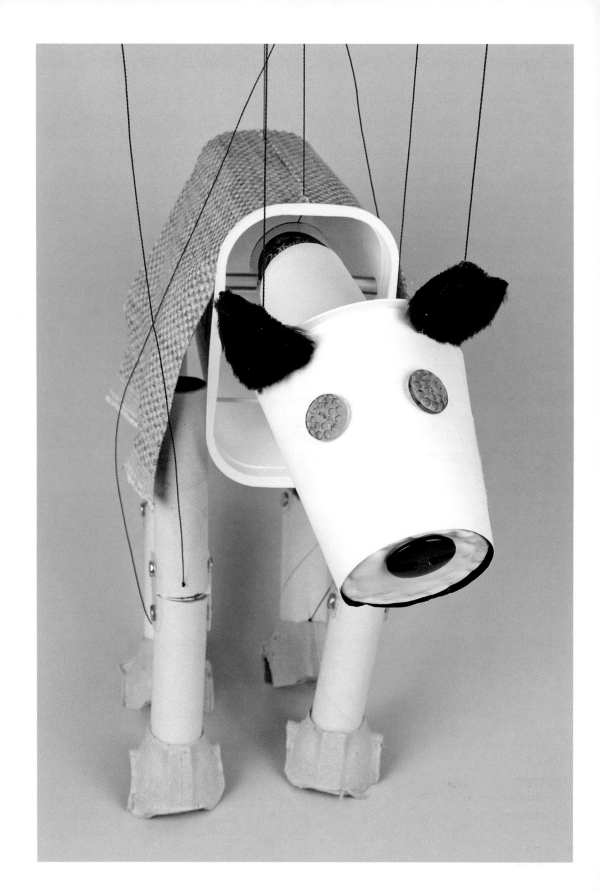

CHAPTER 6

MARIONETTES

The marionettes in this chapter range from simple figures to slightly more complicated structures, though remaining straightforward to make with readily available materials. The puppeteer has less direct control over a marionette than over other puppets, but marionettes have natural, inbuilt movements that the puppeteer can use to their advantage.

This has implications for the method of control; therefore, when planning a marionette, consider the type of control it might require. It is a mistake to make the control too simple unless the puppet has very few strings. Most strings support the puppet and tilting or turning the control achieves a wide range of movements; if the control is too simple, it may be necessary to pull individual strings to effect the required movements, so it is better to let the control do the work for you.

You will find it helpful to read the later section on the principles for stringing a marionette before you proceed to string any of the figures described below.

A SELECTION OF MARIONETTES

A scarf or fabric marionette
This basic marionette demonstrates the power of a puppet. The audience watches little more than a piece of fabric but invests it with character and personality.

OPPOSITE: This marionette donkey has a simple control that is 'paddled' to walk the puppet.

Materials: polystyrene ball or an old ball, large piece of material, wood for the control, thread, trimmings.

1. Make a loop at the end of a piece of thin wire to act like a long needle.
2. Tie a strong thread to the loop and insert the wire through the centre of the ball and out the other side.
3. Insert the needle and thread through the centre of the chosen fabric. The thread should be long enough to reach your waist. Tie the other end of the thread to a small button to prevent it pulling through the ball.

An improvised wire 'needle' is used to thread the head string through a polystyrene ball.

The needle and thread are inserted through the centre of the chosen fabric and the other end is tied to a button to stop it pulling through the ball.

4. Make a control for the marionette by gluing together in a cross two pieces of wood that are suitable for the next stage. Allow the joint to set before using the control.
5. Either drill holes in the control for attaching the control strings, or fix screw-eyes at each end of the control and underneath in the centre.
6. Attach the thread from the ball to the centre underside of the control. It is a good idea at this stage to tie a loose knot in case you need to adjust the length of the thread.
7. Gather the fabric under the ball and tie a piece of cord around it to form the neck.
8. Prepare four long threads to attach near the corners of the fabric. Tie one end of each thread to a small button and, using a needle, insert the threads up through the fabric and tie the ends loosely to the ends of the control.
9. Adjust the length of the threads and, if necessary, reposition where the threads are attached to the fabric, closer to the corners or further away.
10. Experiment with the effects that can be achieved by raising and lowering the central thread, tilting, and turning the control, or picking up separate strings, or pairs of strings.

11. When you are satisfied with the results you can achieve, tie the threads securely to the control and seal the knots with glue.
12. Add features and trimmings as required.

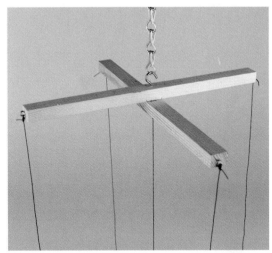

A wooden control is glued together, and the strings attached to the puppet are tied to its centre and the four corners.

After the head string is attached to the control, experiment with the position of the strings on the costume to achieve the desired movements.

Bright, bold features work well on a dark background.

Tilting and turning the control produces limited movements but manipulating individual strings, or pairs of strings, by hand produces a wider range.

A marionette bird from wooden off-cuts

The bird, inspired by an example in John Robert's book, *Making Simple Marionettes*, consists of four pieces of spare wood that needed very little shaping with a rasp and glasspaper to achieve the shapes of a head, a body and feet.

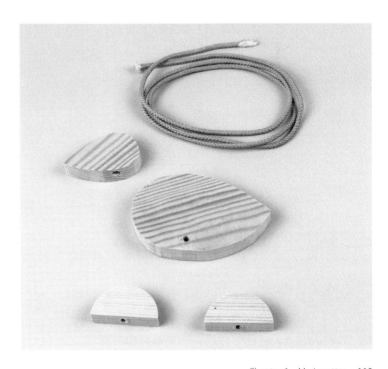

Four wooden off-cuts needed only a little shaping and a few small holes drilled to create the components of this bird.

Materials: wooden off-cuts, cord, wood for the control, thread.

1. Glue the ends of a short cord into holes drilled in a corner of the head and a corresponding corner of the body to form the neck.
2. Drill a hole through the bottom of the body section and insert a continuous length of cord through the hole for the legs. Glue the cord in place, ensuring that the legs are of equal length.
3. Drill holes down through the centre of the feet and glue the ends of the legs into these holes.
4. Glue together two strips of wood to form a cross and drill holes in the four corners (or attach screw-eyes) for attaching the strings. The hook to hang up the puppet may be screwed through the intersection of the cross to strengthen the joint.
5. Attach small screw-eyes to the top of the head and the body.
6. Attach the control strings to the two screw-eyes and to the ankles.
7. Tie the head and body strings to the front and rear of the control respectively and tie the ankle strings to the ends of the cross bar.
8. Add refinements to the bird if you wish, but it is very effective without any additional embellishment.

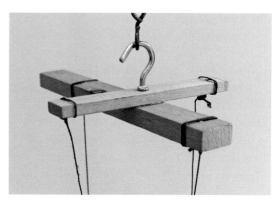

The main bar of the control carries the head at the front and the body towards the end, while the cross bar on the top is for the legs.

Paddling the control produces the walking action. Tilting and turning it controls the head and body.

The assembled puppet ready for stringing.

Rock, tilt and turn the control to move the puppet and use your free hand to move individual strings.

A marionette snake

This marionette is created in the same way as a flexible rod puppet. The head is a polystyrene egg with basic features added and the body is brightly coloured cotton reels threaded on cord and interspaced with small wooden balls or beads. If you use plain cotton reels, you may leave them plain, paint them or cover them with a long tube of a soft material – satins are often suitable for this.

This snake with brightly coloured segments is very effective so no covering material is needed for the body.

Materials: polystyrene egg, cotton reels, small wooden balls, cord, trimmings, long wooden control bar, thread.

1. Make the main flexible body on a central cord, as described in Chapter 5.
2. Make a hole up through the polystyrene egg and thread the central cord up through the hole.
3. Knot the cord on top of the head. Here it is covered by a hat.
4. Tie the tail end of the cord to a small bead.
5. Prepare the control bar by drilling two holes near one end and one hole at the other.

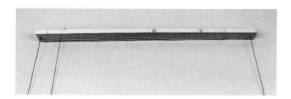

The underside of the control bar shows the holes for threading the head and neck strings and the tail string.

6. Using a needle, thread a continuous control string down through the top of the head and out through the back at the neck.
7. Insert the ends through the two holes at the front of the control bar and tie them to a small bead to make it easier to move them.
8. Tie another long thread to the tail and insert the other end of the thread through the hole in the rear of the control bar. Tie the thread to another bead to enable it to be raised and lowered easily.

Beads attached to the strings on top of the control help with raising and lowering the strings to achieve a variety of body positions.

Hold the control in one hand to tilt and turn the snake and, with the other hand, raise and lower the individual strings or manipulate the strings individually.

Relaxing the tension on the control bar, while manipulating individual strings, adds to the range of movements possible.

A four-legged animal marionette

This puppet, which is a donkey, has plastic cartons for its head and body while the neck and legs are cardboard tubes. They are all hinged together by coat-hanger wire which restricts the head to vertical movements. If it is to turn, then a different joint is needed between the neck and the body, as described for the following puppet.

The construction of the legs and knee joints is detailed fully in Chapter 3. It was an interesting experiment, using whatever materials were at hand. They are not perfect joints but they serve the purpose and demonstrate what can be achieved with a little inventiveness. Note that the front and rear legs should bend in opposite directions.

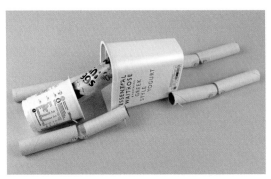

The main parts of the marionette donkey are joined together with horizontal pieces of coat-hanger wire. The front and back legs should bend in opposite directions.

Prepare the control after the puppet is assembled so that you know what size to make the control.

1. Glue together in a cross-shape two strips of wood to control the body and legs. Attach the top piece (the leg bar) about a quarter of the way from the front end of the body control, the main control bar.
2. Make the head control from a piece of dowelling a similar width to the head. Attach a screw-eye in the centre of the dowel and screw a small hook into the front end of the main control to hold the head bar.

3. Drill small holes or fix screw-eyes at each point on the control where strings will be attached.
4. Support the puppet by back strings to the front and rear of the body. Tie each back string to a small button, seal the knot with glue and use a needle to carry the string up through the body to the control.
5. Attach the back strings to the main control near the mid-point and near the end.
6. Attach the head strings in the same way, one to each side of the head, and attach the other ends to the head control.
7. Attach the front leg strings just above the knee and the back leg strings between the knee and the ankle.
8. Note that the front-left and back-right leg strings are attached to the left side of the leg control and the front-right and back-left strings are attached to the right side. This produces the animal's natural walking action.
9. Finish the body with any material and add its features. Here the body has been draped with a 'blanket' which avoids the need to provide other covering and hides the joint between legs and body.

To manipulate the puppet, hold the main control with one hand and rock it in a paddling motion to produce a walking action. Tilt and

The animal control has the longer bar to support the body, a cross bar for the legs, and a head bar hanging from a hook on the front of the control.

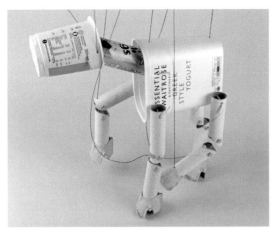

To produce normal walking action, the front left and back right legs are attached at the same point on the control, as are the front right and back left legs.

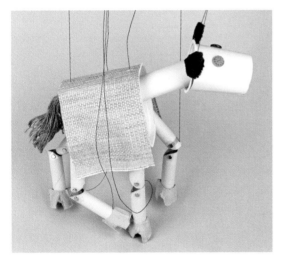

Features, trimmings and a 'blanket' complete the donkey's appearance.

The knee joints were made separately by a method that approximates professional joints reasonably well. These were glued into the upper and lower limbs with suitable packing to hold them securely in place.

Features were added and the puppet was costumed before the strings were attached because it is difficult to add a costume after a puppet has been strung. Most of the costume was glued directly onto the puppet and trimmings were added.

You will see that the legs have been covered but the knees have not. This was a decision of the maker who wanted to see how acceptable this might be. The result was very acceptable and was barely noticed by some of those who saw it in operation.

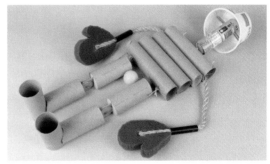

All the elements of this puppet, described in different sections of Chapter 3, are brought together here. The hands are not yet trimmed and shaped.

raise the control for body movements. With your free hand, unhook and move the head control for head movements and use this hand to operate individual strings.

A marionette with human structure

All elements of this marionette's construction are described in Chapters 2 and 3. Most of the body and legs are cardboard tubes with rope arms and foam rubber hands. The carton head is jointed so that it can move in all directions.

When finished and costumed, the character becomes an elderly wizard, or anything else the maker would like him to be.

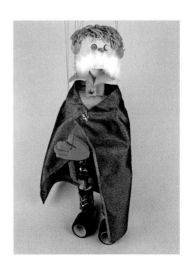

PRINCIPLES FOR STRINGING MARIONETTES

The marionettes in this chapter are all controlled by strong threads, usually black or dark green. In the past, puppeteers often used what was known as No.8 carpet thread, rubbed with beeswax to prevent fraying, but now braided nylon fishing line, intended for fishing carp, is very suitable. I continue to rub these strings with beeswax, but I am not sure that it makes any difference.

Of course, you can use any strong thread you like but it is recommended that you do not use nylon thread or nylon fishing line to try to make the strings less visible. It glistens, drawing attention to itself, and tends to kink when it is wound up to store the puppet. By contrast, black or green thread recedes and is less noticeable when in use.

The string needs to be attached securely to the puppet. Wherever necessary, tie it to a small button inside the relevant part and seal the knot with a spot of glue.

Some of the controls shown have screw-eyes for attaching the strings, while some have holes drilled for this purpose. It is always better *not* to use screw-eyes as these can snag on the strings of other puppets, but this method is shown for the benefit of those who like to unscrew them to sort out any tangles (despite my advice in Chapter 1).

Marionette controls need a hook in the top to hang them up. It is useful to have a few large S-shaped pieces of wire to hang the controls on in case the hooks do not fit where they are to hang. You will find it helpful if you can hang the marionette up when stringing it; attach the head strings to the control and then select a suitable spot to hook the control before proceeding.

The order for stringing is head strings followed by shoulder strings, then hand strings and leg strings. Make the strings long enough for the control to be held at elbow height when the puppet is standing on the performing surface. None of the strings should be too slack.

Head and shoulder strings should have approximately equal tension. To create a stoop or the appearance of aging, slacken the head strings a little so that the head hangs slightly forward.

Hand strings should allow the puppet's hands to hang loosely by its sides when not in use. Where you attach the strings affects how the hands will be positioned, so experiment with different attachment points.

The leg strings should be long enough to allow the puppet to stand straight; attach them just above the knee, ensuring that they do not impede knee movement.

When all strings are attached satisfactorily to the control, tie all knots tightly and seal them with glue.

A detail of the knee joint, showing the leg string attached clear of the joint.

The control described below is a standard upright control that is favoured by many performers, but it is followed by a simpler horizontal control that might suit some people.

MARIONETTE CONTROLS

The methods for controlling animal marionettes will vary with different types of animal, so these have been described above, along with each puppet's construction. For human figures, two main types of control are commonly used; an upright control and a horizontal control, each of which is described below.

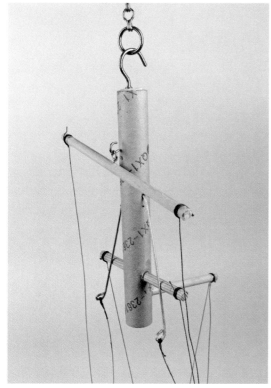

The upright control has a fixed, horizontal head bar, a shoulder bar at the back, hand control wires resting on the head bar, and a detachable leg bar hanging from a hook.

An upright control for human figures

This control would normally be made entirely from wood, but using a strong cardboard tube as the central feature enables quicker construction.

Materials: strong cardboard tube, large diameter dowel, three smaller dowel rods of different lengths, small and large hook, screw-eye, coat-hanger wire, thread.

1. Fix a large hook into the end of a piece of large dowelling (for example a broom handle) which should reach from the top of the control to just before the hand control wires.
2. Glue this dowel into the top of the control.
3. Make holes from side to side across the cardboard tube about 10cm from the bottom and glue the head bar here. The head bar should be a little wider than the head.
4. Make a hole in the back of the cardboard tube a little lower than the head bar. Insert and glue the shoulder bar into this hole. It needs to be long enough to hold the shoulder strings clear of the head, so it may be helpful to make it a little longer than needed and cut any excess away when the stringing is complete.
5. Prepare two pieces of coat-hanger wire for the hand controls. They need to be long enough to rest on the head bar when the top ends are fixed in the control, so make them too long initially. Make a small loop at the end of each wire and seal the loops with a spot of glue.
6. Hold the control with your little finger hooked under the head bar and your other fingers wrapped around the control. Note the position of your index finger and, just above this point, make a small hole right across the control for one of the hand wires. Make a second hole across the control, a little higher still, for the other hand bar; ensure there is sufficient space between the holes for the hand bars not to snag each other.
7. Bend the top of the hand bar into a right angle and insert the end into the prepared hole. Where the wire emerges from the other side of the control, bend it down to secure it and cut off any excess. Repeat the same procedure in the other direction with the other hand bar.
8. Attach a screw-eye in the centre of a longer dowel for the leg bar and screw a small hook into the front of the main control to hold this bar. Ensure that the hook screws into the dowel inside the tubing.
9. Drill small holes through the ends of the leg bar, head bar and shoulder bar.

10. Attach the strings to the control in the order described above, adjust the tensions and when you are satisfied, tie the knots securely and seal them with glue.

To operate the control, hold it in one hand with your little finger under the head bar and your other fingers wrapped around the vertical tubing. Tilt and turn the control to effect head movements. Tilting and turning at the same time will achieve a good head movement.

Unhook the leg bar with your free hand to move the legs. When you walk the puppet, try to keep it standing on the stage surface, not floating or sagging as you do not want it walking in a sitting position. It will help if you can achieve a slight rhythm in the walking.

Use your thumb and index fingers to move the hand wires. When the puppet is standing relatively still, you can use one of the fingers holding the leg bar to move the hand strings individually or together, which will give more varied gestures.

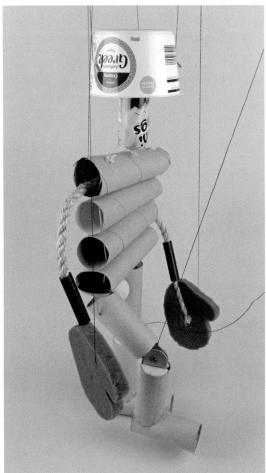

Testing the figure with temporary stringing that needs to be removed before dressing the puppet.

Operating the control with the little finger under the head bar, thumb and index fingers on the hand wires, and free hand for manipulating the leg bar and individual strings.

A horizontal control for human figures

This control has some similarities in its construction to an animal control. Compared with the upright control, it is quicker to make and simpler to operate with little practice but the range of movements possible is more limited, except in very skilful hands.

Materials: two pieces of wood and three dowel rods, hook, screw-eyes.

A horizontal control for human figures consists of a leg bar glued across the top of the main bar and (from right to left) a hand control bar on a hook, a head bar and a shoulder bar, both suspended on cord.

1. Glue together in a cross-shape two strips of wood as the main control bar and the leg bar. Attach the top piece (the leg bar) towards the front end of the main bar.
2. Use cord, with screw-eyes or drilled holes, to suspend two dowel rods from the control. The head bar is suspended approximately in the centre of the control. The shoulder bar is near the back and should be wide enough to keep the shoulder strings clear of the head.
3. A dowel rod for the hand bar is hung on a hook at the front of the control.
4. Insert screw-eyes, or drill small holes, in the ends of the three dowel rods and the leg bar. Attach the puppet's strings to these points while following the principles outlined above.
5. As an alternative to the hand bar, make the hand strings from a continuous loop of thread and hang this on the front hook.

Tilt and turn the main control to move the puppet and paddle it for walking. Use your free hand to move the head and shoulder bars and to control the hand strings.

Storage

When marionettes are not in use and you need to hang them up or lay them down without tangling, gather the strings together and wind them around a slotted 'winder' that can be made from thick card or a thin piece of wood, such as MDF or plywood.

A slotted winder used to keep the strings from tangling when not in use or in storage.

CHAPTER 7

SHADOW PUPPETS

S hadow puppets may take any shape and form that you choose, but it is common practice to create human figures with the head in profile and the body slightly turned, rather than having a side-on view of the whole figure. This convention can be seen from early Asian figures through to today.

For the basic silhouette, collect many types of opaque cardboard. It does not have to be black card, but it should be thick enough to stay stiff yet not so thick that cutting is difficult. Cereal boxes or cardboard envelopes are about the right thickness and can be strengthened by a coating of PVA medium if necessary. Plastic and translucent sheets are useful too. Large, thick cardboard boxes are suitable for making shadow stages.

Translucent coloured acetate, tissue paper and cellophane all enhance shadow puppets that have cut-out designs with colourful inserts.

Translucent figures in full colour are created on white card with water-based felt pens, dyes, or radiant, concentrated water colours. Spirit-based pens can be used but, over time, the colours tend to blend into each other; for the first few weeks it looks very subtle but eventually the effect is spoiled.

The best card to use is Ivory Board weighing 335g per square metre for figures up to 60cm. When selecting an alternative card, look for a similar thickness, up to 400gsm; thin card will be too floppy and thick card will be harder to make translucent.

Different types of cardboard, and some plastic sheets, collected for making shadows and scenery.

Coloured tissue paper, acetates and cellophane bring colour to shadow puppets, though simple black images on a white screen can be very refreshing.

Materials for creating shadows in full colour: a variety of water-based felt pens, highlighters and bottles of concentrated radiant watercolours.

OPPOSITE: A shadow of a puppet, cut in the style of Lotte Reiniger as an exercise, with the head in profile and the body turned.

SIMPLE SHADOW PUPPETS

A human figure

You can create this figure directly on to a sheet of cardboard, but it is often helpful to make a paper template first.

Materials: pencil, sheet of paper, cardboard.

1. Sketch and cut out the design for the puppet on paper.
2. Draw around this template on a sheet of card.
3. Cut out the figure with scissors or a sharp knife on a cutting board.
4. Add one of the controls detailed below, with the plain side facing the screen.

A sketched figure is cut out to use as a template for a puppet.

The cut-out figure needs no moving parts.

The reverse side of the card reveals that it was from a cereal box. Keep the plain side facing the screen as the printed side might show through it.

The simple figure is more striking as a shadow than the shape that creates it.

An animal figure
Follow the same procedures to make a shadow puppet animal.

A paper template of a horse is used to draw the outline for this figure.

The cardboard figure is cut out.

The shadow created by the horse.

DETAIL AND DECORATION

Cut-out design

Shadow puppets can be enhanced by cutting out a little detail from the figure. Avoid cutting away too much or it will weaken the puppet; if necessary, strengthening is possible with wire or clear acetate glued or taped on. When planning the design, consider where you will attach the control.

Materials: pencil, paper, cardboard.

1. Draw and cut out the design on paper, then trace around this onto the selected card.
2. Cut out the design with scissors and/or a sharp blade. Small scissors with sharp points and a paper drill or a paper punch are useful for this.
3. Add a control, as detailed below and the puppet is ready to use.

A paper template with a cut-out design is used to trace the details onto card.

The cardboard figure is ready to be used.

The image of the female character becomes sharper when it is tight against the screen but, depending on the light source, the shadows tend to be slightly softer as the puppets perform.

Detail and colour

Detail and colour can be introduced into shadow puppets with cut-out designs, using a range of textured or coloured translucent materials.

Materials: pencil, paper, cardboard, glue or tape, coloured acetate or cellophane or tissue paper, textured material.

1. Cut out the design as before.
2. On the side of the puppet that faces the operator, glue or tape the textured material over the cut-out sections. The texture will show on the shadow.
3. Experiment with different materials as some will provide a crisper texture than others.
4. To introduce colour in the decoration, glue or tape the coloured material over the cut-out sections.
5. Colour and texture can also be used together.

Textured material is taped to the back of the puppet.

The audience sees the textured shadows.

Coloured acetate taped on the figure and the effect on the screen.

Coloured effects with blue tissue paper and pale blue cellophane.

Coloured acetate and textured material were combined for this figure.

ARTICULATED SHADOW PUPPETS

Shadow puppets that have a fixed pose are a readily accepted convention, but figures with separate, jointed parts have considerable scope and are interesting to watch.

It must be remembered that additional moving parts can mean extra controls, so how many hands would be needed to operate a single puppet with multiple joints? The solution is to limit the number of joints and the number of controls but have a few moving parts that have interesting poses. You may be surprised at what can be achieved with a single control attached to the body. Use the action of the puppet against the screen to help control the figure and, once again, let the imagination of the audience work for you.

The principles for making articulated shadow puppets are the same for human and animal figures. They have different shapes, limbs, and where they are attached may be different, but the joints are made in the same way. Arrange the jointed parts so that they do not impede each other. Often this means attaching them to different sides of the main structure.

The Joints

The most common methods for joints are rivet-type paper fasteners (also known as split pins), knotted thread and splayed cord that is untwisted and glued flat against the separate parts.

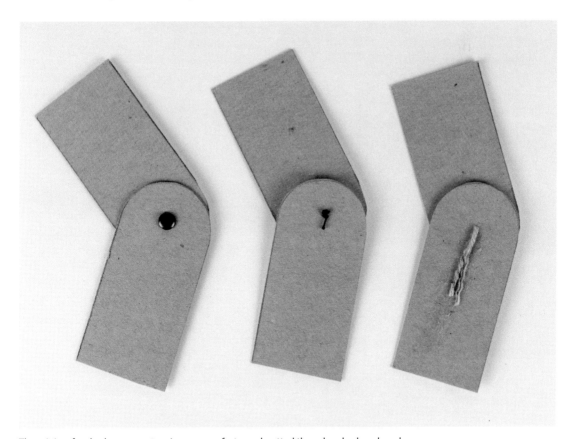

Three joints for shadow puppets using a paper fastener, knotted thread and splayed cord.

Paper fasteners are the quickest and easiest method. Punch holes in the parts to be joined, insert the fasteners and open them out flat on the other side. The joint should be quite tight but moving freely.

Knotted thread gives the smoothest movement between parts but is a fiddlier method. Insert a needle with strong thread through the overlapping parts and tie off each end very close to the card. Add further knots to ensure the thread cannot pull through the joint. Press the knots as flat as possible and seal them with a spot of glue.

Splayed cord glued down is satisfactory and sits somewhere between the other two methods in terms of convenience.

Restricted Joints

If a joint bends in the wrong direction, this might not matter but, if necessary, it can be restricted with a short piece of thread inserted into the jointed parts and knotted. You may need to experiment with the length and positioning of the thread.

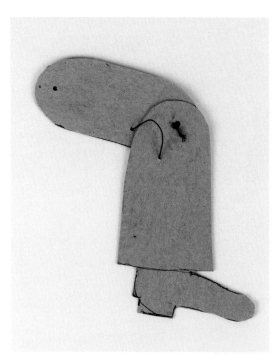

A short piece of thread attached to each of the parts does not restrict bending.

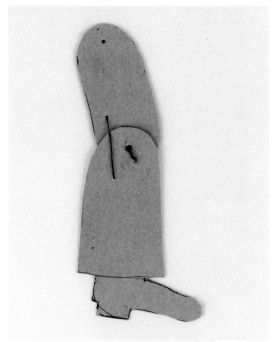

The thread limits the movement of the joint, stopping it from bending in the wrong direction.

An Articulated Shadow Puppet

Materials: pencil, paper, cardboard, paper fasteners or thread or cord.

1. Design the figure on paper, identifying where the joints will be.
2. Use this template to redraw on paper and cut out the parts separately.
3. Transfer the separate paper templates onto card and cut out all the pieces.
4. Use paper fasteners, thread, or cord to join the moving parts to the main character.
5. Add a control, as detailed below.

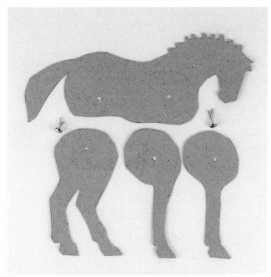

The horse is cut in cardboard with punched holes carefully placed ready for the joints.

The template for an articulated figure identifies when the legs will overlap the body.

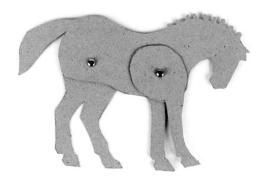

Paper fasteners are used to attach the legs on separate sides of the body.

A second paper template is prepared with the separate parts cut out.

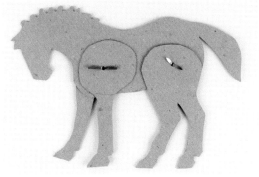

On the reverse side, the prongs of the paper fasteners are pressed flat, taking care not to make them too tight or they will restrict the leg movements.

SHADOW PUPPETS IN FULL COLOUR

The puppet illustrated is an unarticulated figure. If it is to be jointed, design the figure with the separated parts, allowing for the areas that overlap in the same way as the previous example. Do not cut out the separate parts until it has all been coloured, oiled and wiped clean at the end of the sequence below.

The effect will appear stronger if you colour the side that will face the screen. If you use concentrated radiant water colours, like this example, you need only a few drops of each colour which you can use full strength, diluted in varying strengths, or mixed with other colours. You can achieve a considerable variety of shades and colours by dilutions and mixtures of Turquoise Blue, Daffodil Yellow and Tropic Pink.

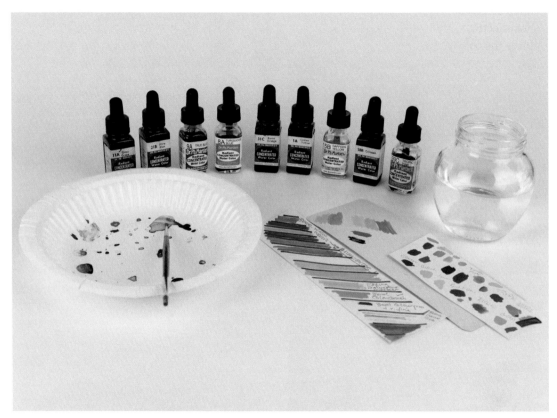

Concentrated radiant water colours with colour-tests; only a single drop from a bottle is needed in most cases. Mixing and diluting is done with a brush on the paper plate.

Making coloured shadow puppets

Materials: white card, pencil, colouring pens or inks, clear liquid paraffin or cooking oil, paper towel.

1. Design the puppet and transfer the design lightly onto thin white card. The example has been given a bold, black outline of all parts but this is not essential; the colouring can be more subtle without such lines, if you wish.
2. Colour the entire figure, ensuring that you fill in all blocks of colour; light shading is not effective.
3. Place the coloured card on a paper towel on a protected work surface.
4. Oil the card with a piece of paper towel soaked in cooking oil or liquid paraffin, which is cleaner. Soak the card effectively without flooding it. It will be noticeably transparent already.
5. Repeat the oiling on the other side of the card until the colour shows through.
6. Hold the card up to the light; any areas not sufficiently oiled will appear slightly grey or darker.
7. When the oiling is complete, use a fresh paper towel to wipe any excess oil from both sides of the card.
8. Cut out the figure. If there are any fragile parts, like the antennae of this butterfly, leave some of the oiled white card attached to them or they will break.

A butterfly is drawn in black outline, though it can be sketched lightly in pencil that will not show, if that is preferred.

The butterfly design is filled with solid colour – no shading or white spaces.

The coloured card is oiled to make it translucent; the darker areas show where less oiling has occurred.

The reverse side is oiled fully and excess oil is wiped off to avoid oiling the screen.

SHADOW PUPPET CONTROLS

The control used for a shadow puppet depends upon where you will be positioned to operate it, which is influenced by the source of light, as detailed in Chapter 8. You usually need to hold the puppet close against the shadow screen, so operation from directly behind or from below at an angle suits most purposes. The best arrangement is a control hinged to the puppet so operation can be at any angle necessary.

A further consideration is where and how you will store the puppets and whether the figures can be placed flat or whether the control needs to be removed to do so.

Attach the main control rod just above the puppet's point of balance so that it has a natural tendency to remain upright. Otherwise, it will be trying to turn over all the time you are operating it.

A Dowel Rod Control

This is probably the simplest form of control, though it is not the best. A dowel rod is attached

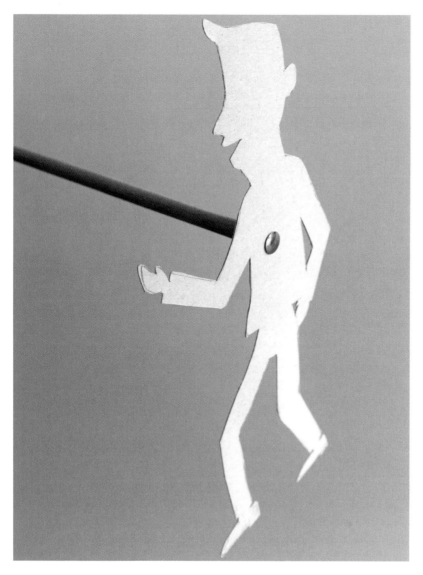

A horizontal control with the puppet fixed to a dowel rod with a drawing pin.

horizontally to the puppet and secured with a drawing pin pushed in tightly from the other side. If it works loose, just tap the drawing pin to tighten it.

You need to work from directly behind the puppet, which is manageable when performing by daylight or fluorescent light, but other light sources might not be so easy.

When not in use, place the rods on a shelf or on the edge of a table so that the figures can stand undisturbed. If you need to lay the figures down, you need to remove the drawing pin after every use which adds to their wear.

An alternative is to use small pieces of Velcro tape with the fuzzy surface glued or stapled to the puppet and the spikey surface glued on the end of the rod. Press the Velcro together for use but separate them carefully for storage.

A Garden Stake

This is a cheap alternative to using dowelling for the control. Glue and tape an L-shaped piece of wire (for example part of a paper clip) to the wooden stake and tape the other end of the wire to the puppet. It is a simple method that will allow you to hold the control at any convenient angle to perform.

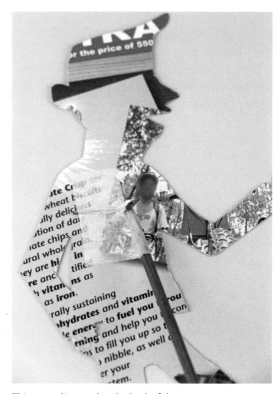

This control is taped to the back of the puppet.

A Hinged Wire Control

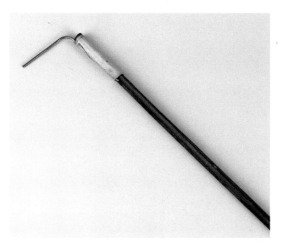

A piece of wire is glued and taped to a plant stake for a simple control at any angle.

The recommended method, with the control hinged to the puppet.

This is the recommended method as it is secure, easy to store, gives excellent control, and enables operation from any angle.

Make an elongated loop at the end of a piece of coat-hanger wire and attach it to the puppet with a strip of card glued on either side of the loop but not on the wire.

When using full-colour shadow puppets, replace the strip of card with clear acetate and use a clear contact glue, such as UHU. Also ensure that you thoroughly wipe the surface of the puppet to remove any oil.

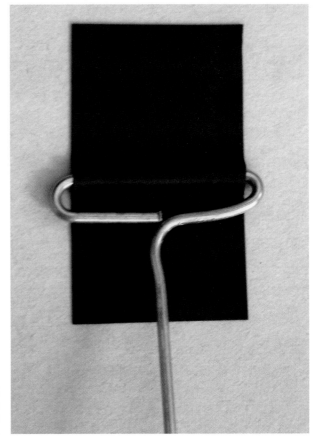

Another view of the hinged control for clarity. Card (or clear acetate for full-colour puppets) is glued to the puppet on either side of the loop of wire.

Additional Controls

If any extra controls are required, for example for moving arms or hands, it is a good idea to control them with a length of coat-hanger wire. Make a small loop in the end of the wire, seal the knot with glue, and attach the loop to the jointed part with strong thread.

If extra controls are required, a loop in the end of the control wire is attached to the moving part with thread.

Handles for Controls

Handling wire controls is much easier if they are fixed into wooden handles. Carefully drill a small hole down into a piece of dowelling and glue the end of the control into the hole. The hole should be a tight fit or the handle may become loose.

The hinged control, set in a dowel handle, enables operation from any angle, which is useful when organising the positions of the performers and the source of light.

CHAPTER 8

STAGING AND PERFORMING

STAGING

The 'stage' here means the space in which you are to perform. It can be as simple as performing from behind a piece of furniture, behind a screen, on a table-top, or inside a purpose-made stage. Or you might perform 'open-stage', which means out in the open, in view of the audience, which is quite common practice.

Whichever type of staging you adopt, have regard for its size. Five puppets on stage might mean up to five performers fitting backstage, and the height of any screen will influence whether the performers need to crouch, stretch, or can perform comfortably.

Consider the background against which the puppets will be seen. The audience will focus on the puppets and will ignore even a busy background, but it will enhance the performance if the background is a plain wall, a screen or some form of scene.

A Simple Screen
This screen consists of a piece of thick fabric looped over a thick dowel, such as a broom handle. It is suspended between the backs of two chairs or the ends of a table. It works equally well in front of a plain wall or another draped fabric.

A Cardboard Stage
This is a very flexible stage made from a large cardboard box. It can be used on a table-top for hand and rod puppets, on the floor for marionettes or adapted to become a shadow screen. It folds up easily for storage, which is always a consideration with stages.

Cut the top and one of the long sides from the box and open out the remaining three sides to make the stage. You can use it either way round and can leave it plain or decorate the parts that face the audience.

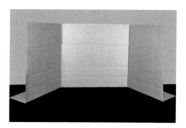

Removing the top and one side from a large box is a quick way to create a stage. Decorate it in any way you like.

Draped fabric on a rod suspended between two chairs can be used for hand, rod and string puppets.

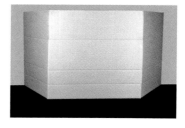

The stage can be used either way around, on a table-top or on the floor.

OPPOSITE: Rehearsing a table-top puppet. The controls are normally black but are kept light here for clarity.

Scenery for the cardboard stage

Cut-out cardboard scenery can be fitted into scenery slots.

1. Draw and cut out the scenery on stiff card, leaving a significant rectangular tag at the bottom.
2. Prepare a long strip of strong card and two short pieces of the same height.
3. Glue the short pieces onto each end of the long strip. The distance between them should be the same as the width of the tag on the scenery.
4. Glue the scenery slot inside the top edge of the stage and insert the scenery into it.
5. Add any additional scenery you need but remember that large scenery may reduce the playing area.

Cut-out scenery with a tag at the bottom to fit into a scenery slot.

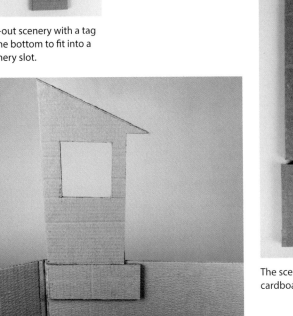

Making a scenery slot with two cardboard blocks glued onto the ends of a longer cardboard strip.

The scenery tag should fit smoothly between the cardboard blocks.

The scenery slot is glued inside the top of the stage to accommodate the scenery tag.

Stage Drapes

If you are not using scenery with the stage, you can cover it with suitable drapes but have regard also for the appearance of the surface on which the stage is standing. The images show the stage covered in a plain jersey material, standing on velvet fabric, and the stage in use for hand and rod puppets performing against a plain background.

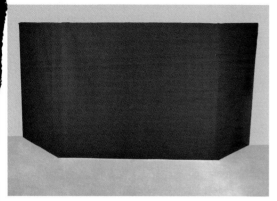

The stage can be draped with fabric of a suitable colour when scenery is not attached.

A marionette can perform in front of the drape-covered stage.

The stage in use for hand and rod puppets with the puppeteers hidden behind it.

TABLE-TOP PERFORMING

A table-top, suitably draped, can be a stage to hide the operators, and the table itself provides a useful surface on which to stand any props.

However, table-top performing usually means using the table as the playing surface with the operators in view of the audience. Professional performers would often be dressed entirely in black, with hoods that they can see through, sometimes with the puppets held in carefully directed beams of light so that the performers are almost invisible, but the participants had a more relaxed approach for exploring possibilities here.

The playing surface is a decorator's folding pasting table covered with a plain jersey fabric. The background is a drape suspended from a pole. Operation of the puppets requires a coordinated approach to operate the head, body, arms and legs, whether via controls or directly moving the puppet by hand.

A table-top used as a playboard for a rod puppet.

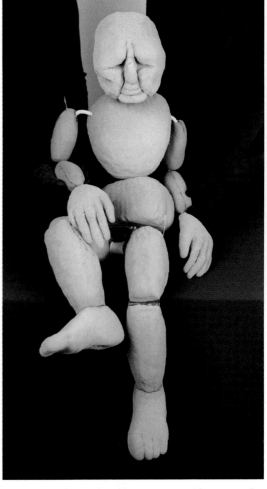

Exploring co-ordinated manipulation of a table-top puppet by two performers.

Direct manipulation of a table-top puppet without control rods is readily accepted by an audience.

MARIONETTES

The images for marionette staging all make use of the same draped material that is shown earlier suspended between two chairs. It may be suspended on poles of any length and either gathered up or spread out.

The rehearsal image of the wizard shows one style of open-stage performing where the performer can appear close to, or even among an audience. The image of the ghostly penguin demonstrates open stage performing where the performer is visible but behind a waist-high screen that provides a background for the puppets.

The final images in this section are a reminder of the before-and-after appearance of the wizard and you will see that even the basic puppet, without features or costume, can have a commanding presence on a stage.

Open-stage performing with the puppeteer in full view of the audience offers scope for more creative use of space.

An alternative form of open-stage performance with the puppeteer operating over a backscreen but visible above waist height.

This puppet has a commanding presence on stage, even without features or costume.

The costume and features change the appearance and character of the puppet.

SHADOW PUPPET STAGING

Shadow play is one of the quickest and easiest forms of puppet theatre to create and, contrary to popular belief, it is not essential to have a darkened room, blackouts, or even artificial lighting. Some of the most captivating performances I have seen have been in classrooms with natural light through the windows.

The playing surface for shadows is normally a screen, though they can be played on a wall or other surface, depending on the source and strength of the light. For most purposes a plain white screen is suitable, as described under 'Materials' in Chapter 2.

Improvised Shadow Screens

A picture frame screen

The screen here is polyester cotton. It may be taped, pinned or stapled inside a picture frame that is propped up in a suitable position, leaning very slightly forward.

A shadow screen fixed in a picture frame.

To make the screen more permanent, attach L-shaped brackets to it and screw these to a piece of timber wide enough to provide stability, such as an old shelf.

A shower curtain screen
A plain shower curtain makes an excellent screen. The whole screen, or a section cut from it, can be hung from a pole, pinned or stapled to a piece of timber (top and bottom), or attached to a wooden frame and made stable like the picture frame.

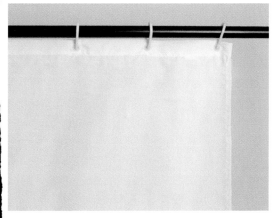

A shower curtain suspended from a pole can be a very large screen or it can be shielded with drapes to reduce the performing area.

A Cardboard Shadow Stage

This is the same cardboard stage as described earlier, amended to contain a shadow screen and shadow scenery. It can continue to be used for other types of puppet with the stage and screen covered by draped fabric.

Materials: greaseproof paper, strips of cardboard, adhesive tape.

1. Having removed the top and one long side from the box, carefully cut a rectangular hole from the remaining long section. Leave sufficient space below and beside the hole to accommodate the scenery slots and any lighting that you might use.

2. Use strong adhesive tape to attach the screen on the inside of the stage. This example uses greaseproof paper cut from a kitchen roll.

A rectangle is cut from the cardboard stage to introduce a shadow screen.

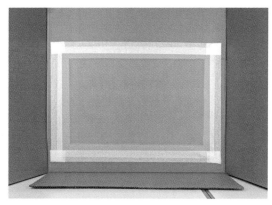

The screen is taped to the stage on the performer's side.

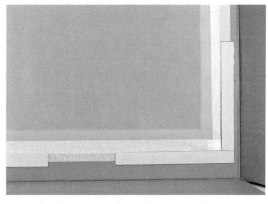

Strips of card are attached near the corners of the screen.

3. Cut four narrow strips of cardboard about the same thickness as any scenery you might use. Glue these strips of cardboard in an L-shape to each side of the screen at the bottom and a reasonable distance from the hole (*see* page 151).

4. Cut four wider strips of strong card and glue the bottom edges on top of the narrow strips so that the wider strips do not overlap the hole for the screen. These are the scenery slots in which any shadow scenery can be held and changed during a performance.

Scenery

Any scenery on a shadow screen reduces the playing area, unless the scenery is translucent, so keep scenery to the minimum necessary to establish the scene. As with the puppets, the scenery may be solid card or card with cut-out shapes and added coloured or textured areas. When designing the scenery, plan to leave extra card at the bottom to fit into the scenery slots.

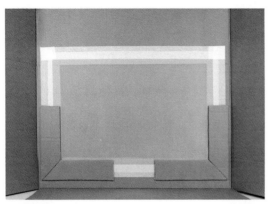

Wider strips of card are glued to the narrow strips to create scenery slots.

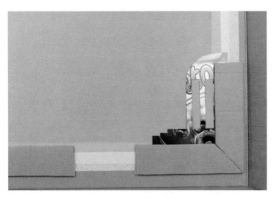

Scenery in the scenery slot is held tightly against the screen.

A rear-view of the cardboard scenery with coloured acetate taped on. It is extended at the side and bottom to fit into the scenery slot.

LIGHT FOR SHADOW PLAY

Shadow play can be created by daylight, with a simple or a powerful light source or with fluorescent lighting, but the type and position of the lighting will influence your operating position. Whether you sit, kneel or stand behind the screen, ensure that you are comfortable, especially if you plan to rehearse or perform for long periods.

Some sources of light will illuminate the screen evenly while others will light certain parts of the screen more intensely, but this is accepted as the nature of shadow play.

Whatever source of light you use, avoid having the light shining into the audience through the screen.

Daylight

To perform by daylight, set up the screen with the operator's side close to a window. This will provide an even, diffuse light and clear shadows, provided that the puppets are held against the screen. If they drift away from the screen, the shadows will disappear, but this is a feature that can be used deliberately to advantage in a performance.

A backstage view of performing by daylight.

When performing by daylight, the controls and the puppeteers will not cast shadows on the screen but avoid direct sunlight as it will cast heavy shadows of everything, including the window frames.

Shadows by daylight. There are no shadows of the controls, nor the puppeteer.

Coloured shadows are also clear in daylight.

Domestic lighting

Many types of domestic light are suitable. Even a strong torch can be used but, for convenience, a light that can be clipped onto the stage or to a nearby object, or a free-standing, adjustable light such as a reading lamp, will serve the purpose. This will enable you to arrange a suitable way to position the light and avoid casting your own shadow on the screen. Frosted or pearl bulbs will give a more satisfactory light than clear ones.

Performing with domestic lighting may not illuminate the screen evenly but this is the charm of traditional shadow play.

Powerful electric light

Powerful light sources, such as overhead projectors, slide projectors and strong spotlights offer various possibilities for playing with light and the shadows will stay strong and enlarge if they move away from the screen. However, such lighting poses its own issues such as angles and avoiding distortion, lights shining directly at the audience and finding the best operating position for the puppeteers, but it is an option that will suit some circumstances.

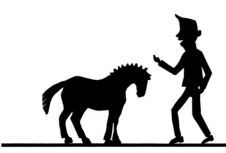

Shadows with powerful lights allow play with size and scale by changing the distance between puppet and screen.

Fluorescent striplights

A fluorescent striplight placed behind the screen provides a reasonable diffuse light and does not cast shadows of the performers nor the controls. It is available in different powers and lengths and can be attached to a suitable base for stability. A particular advantage is that it remains cool.

Adjust the distance between the light and the screen to achieve even illumination and the strongest shadows. Coloured sheets of acetate (lighting gels) can safely be laid over the light to achieve coloured lighting effects.

Fluorescent lights remain cool which is a great help. Adjust the distance between the light and screen to achieve the most even illumination.

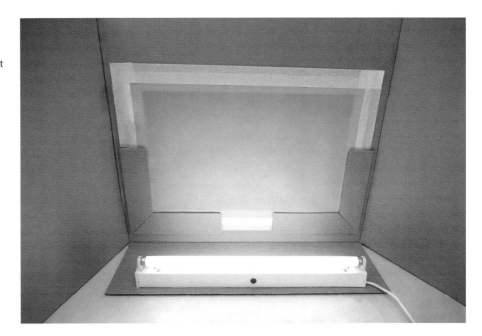

Coloured lighting gels (acetates) can be safely rested over fluorescent lights.

Backstage, performing with fluorescent lighting.

An exercise in Lotte Reiniger-style images presented with fluorescent light.

HE PERFORMANCE

he 'performance' may take any form you wish.
does not have to be a scripted play; it might
be a song, a poem, a folk tale, a fairy story, a
humorous sketch, a favourite story, or one you
have created yourself. Popular classical music
can also provide inspiration for a performance.
You might have a scenario, an outline of the
action, and improvise around that. Starting with
a simple story, or a song that tells a story, is an
excellent way to get started, build confidence
and discover the potential of puppets.

There are a few key areas to consider when
planning a performance. First, your audience:
for whom will you be performing, how old are
they and what will interest them? If it is a play,
remember that good plays for humans are often
not good puppet plays, especially if they have
too much dialogue and too little action. It is
better to start with a story, consider how much
can be translated into action, and build upon
that. At what point in a story should your performance open and what elements are essential?
Delete events that do not advance the story or
the characterisation and, having outlined the
key elements, consider how you will conclude
the piece effectively. Avoid stating 'The End'.

Shadow play is not suited to long speeches but
works well with short episodes, narration, and a
mixture of narration and speech. It can also be
used as a background for other types of puppet,
for linking narrative or dream sequences.

Avoid shrill, squeaky voices and sloppy dialogue; try speaking for the puppet in your own
formal voice and then experiment with different
character voices. Find a character voice for each
puppet that suits both you and the puppet.

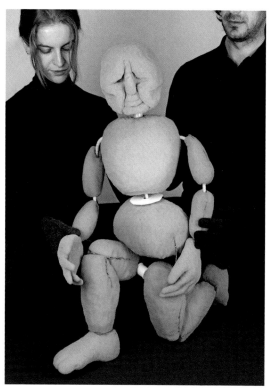

This character was created with a view to performing
Samuel Beckett's *Act Without Words*.

The stillness
of a puppet,
or a tilt of the
head, can evoke
an emotional
response from
an audience.

Starting with a familiar short story is one way to get started.

Try to achieve a variety of pace and emotion and keep the audience interested in what is coming next. Avoid long speeches, long scene changes (maximum two to three minutes), and long performances. A few short pieces may be better received than one long one.

Good manipulation requires concentration. Maintain the same focus as your puppet and look where the puppet looks, as if you are seeing through the puppet's eyes. Explore the use of space and consider how your puppets relate to each other. How do we know which one is speaking? Do not over-emphasise the movement of the puppet that is speaking by jerking the puppet's head to every word, but combine controlled head movements with appropriate gestures. Subdue the movements of the other puppets so that they appear to be listening thoughtfully, but are not lifeless.

Do not rush the manipulation; make the actions deliberate and carefully timed. Avoid unnecessary movements and make every gesture as crisp and clean as possible. Try to achieve variation of gesture within a puppet's characterisation and let the puppet's natural movements do as much as possible for you. Always keep the puppets in character; when they enter and leave the stage, they should not swing into place nor pop up behind a screen.

Allow adequate time for rehearsal before presenting your performance and, if it is a group activity, everyone should know their roles thoroughly. Arrange fixed places for figures, props and scenery so that they can be identified immediately when needed. Sometimes you might need to choreograph the movements of the performers backstage to ensure smooth movements of the puppets on stage.

After a couple of performances, review how they were received. What reaction did you get from the audience? What went particularly well? Were there any parts when they seemed a little restless? Did they laugh at the funny parts or at parts that were not intended to be funny? What did you learn from this and would you do anything differently another time?

Most of all, enjoy your puppetry!

Throughout history puppets have been able to speak the unspeakable.

Let me see the puppet think.

NDEX

159

First published in 2024 by
The Crowood Press Ltd
Ramsbury, Marlborough
Wiltshire SN8 2HR

enquiries@crowood.com
www.crowood.com

British Library Cataloguing-in-Publication Data
A catalogue record for this book is available from
the British Library.

ISBN 978 0 7198 4397 6

Cover design by Sergey Tsvetkov
All photography is by David Currell

Front cover: A finger puppet inspired by
Thomasina Smith's book, *Fantastic Finger Puppets
to Make Yourself* (Barnes & Noble, 2014)

Typeset by SJmagic DESIGN SERVICES, India.
Printed and bound in India by Nutech Print Services - India

ACKNOWLEDGEMENTS

I am indebted to all the puppeteers, teachers
and therapists who have shared their ideas and
experience over many years. My particular
thanks are due to my friend and colleague,
Sue Miles-Pearson, Senior Lecturer and Lead
Tutor in Primary Design and Technology at
the School of Primary Education, University of
Roehampton, for her involvement, ideas and
advice at every stage in preparing this book.

Thanks are due also to my friend Mark
Heald, for his expert advice on photography,
and to Can Bakay and my daughter, Emily
Currell, for their help with the final chapters.

Once again, thank you to the team at
Crowood who produce such beautiful books. It
is always a pleasure to work with them.